THE
LITTLE
BOOK
OF
SUFFOLK

NEIL R. STOREY

The
History
Press

First published in 2013
Reprinted in 2017
This paperback edition printed in 2020

The History Press
97 St George's Place, Cheltenham,
Gloucestershire, GL50 3QB
www.thehistorypress.co.uk

British Library Cataloguing in publication Data
A catalogue record for this book is available from the British Library

ISBN 978 0 7509 9512 2

Typesetting and orignation by The History Press
Printed and bound by TJ International, Padstow, Cornwall

 Trees for LYfe

CONTENTS

ACKNOWLEDGEMENTS

I would like to thank my friends for sharing their knowledge of and suggestions for subjects, and all those kind historians, staff and volunteers in museums, heritage centres and libraries across the county who have kindly helped me with my research. Particular thanks are due to Andrew Selwyn-Crome, Stewart P. Evans, Alan Murdie, Ivan Bunn, Chris Reeve, James Nice, Martin Faulks, Richard Blake, Sue Tod, Archivist at Felixstowe Museum, the Long Shop Museum, Leiston, Ipswich Museum, Moyse's Hall Museum, Bury St Edmunds, Ron Carr and Tony Slatter at HMS *Ganges* Association Museum, Landguard Fort, Dr Stephen Cherry, Alan Kempton, Andy Jennings, Jenny Phillips, Sophie Dunn, Michelle Bullivant, Robert Green, Treasure Chest Books, JC Books of Watton, the late John Timpson, Joy and all the Suffolk-born branch of clan Storey. And last but certainly not least, my loving family.

INTRODUCTION

Suffolk is a very special county with rolling acres of mellow countryside and beautiful coastline, punctuated with many villages and towns of unspoilt charm and heritage. The county's landscape, history, nature, skies, sunsets and people continue to inspire generations of artists, musicians and writers both born and bred or new to the county. To know Suffolk is to love it; the character of the county immerses both visitor and local alike, but how many people really know the county? This book does not pretend to be a history, concise almanac or guide; instead, it is a collection of the ephemeral, miscellaneous and quirky facts about Suffolk that you didn't know you wanted to know until now.

Armed with this volume, the intrepid reader will be able to discover such gems of knowledge as:

Who was the man known as Bilious Bale?

What was Oliver Cromwell's disembodied head doing at Woodbridge?

Where was the last invasion landing by foreign troops in England?

When was the first recorded race run at Newmarket?

How tall is the tower of St Edmundsbury Cathedral?

Why is there a house 60ft in the air at Orford Ness?

The contents of this book will enliven any conversation or quiz. It may even give pause to those who know and love Suffolk to say, 'Well, fancy that!'

Neil R. Storey, 2013

1

ABOUT SUFFOLK

The name of the county comes from after the Saxons and Anglos divided Britain into kingdoms and the foundation of East Anglia in AD 575. Those in the north of the new kingdom were soon known as the North-folk and those in the south, the South-folk; this was soon corrupted to Suffolk. Although this name for the locality was in use for many years previously, the earliest written reference to Suffolk found to date was in AD 1045.

The administrative county of Suffolk covers 1,466 square miles.

Suffolk shares its borders with Norfolk to the north, Essex to the south, Cambridgeshire to the west and the North Sea to the east.

Suffolk is the most easterly county of England.

According to the Office for National Statistics, in 2011 the population of Suffolk was 730,100 and rated as the thirty-second largest county population in England. It has a population density of 192 per square kilometre and ranks as the thirty-eighth county for population density.

The county of Suffolk covers 1,467 square miles and ranks as the eighth largest ceremonial county of England.

At its greatest length, Suffolk is 52 miles across.

At its greatest breadth, Suffolk measures 48 miles.

Much of Suffolk is low-lying and founded on Pleistocene sand and clays. It is only the west of the county that stands on the more resistant Cretaceous chalk.

The soil of Suffolk varies, but a strong loam on clay marl bottom, ideal for agriculture, predominates throughout the county.

The Red Crag geological deposit reaches a depth of 147ft at Southwold.

The highest point of the county is Great Wood Hill, on the Newmarket Ridge near Rede. It has an elevation of 420ft.

Lowestoft is the most easterly town in the county and therefore the United Kingdom.

Ness Point, also known as Lowestoft Ness, is the most easterly place in the United Kingdom.

The Suffolk coastline is mostly bordered by heathland known as the Sandlings.

The Suffolk Coast and Heaths, an Area of Outstanding Natural Beauty, stretches over 60 miles from Kessingland to the Shotley Peninsula, and encompasses 155 square miles of wetlands, heaths, beaches, towns and villages.

Alton Water Reservoir is the largest area of inland water in the county. Opened in 1987, the construction work and completion took thirteen years. The pumping station and water treatment works below the dam is capable of treating 10 million imperial gallons of water a day.

In 2005, there was a discovery of flint tools in the cliffs at Pakefield, and as a result the human habitation of the Lowestoft area can now be traced back 700,000 years.

When the Orwell Bridge was opened in 1982 it was one of the largest pre-stressed concrete structures in Europe.

The Port of Felixstowe is the largest container port in the United Kingdom.

In 1929, there were a total of 503 civil parishes in the county of Suffolk.

The parish of Dallinghoo Wield, which covered just 34 acres, was claimed as the smallest parish in England until 1980 when it was declared an anachronism by the boundary commissioners and abolished as a parish in its own right.

East Suffolk, West Suffolk and Ipswich were merged to form the unified county of Suffolk on 1 April 1974, under the Local Government Act 1972.

Today, Suffolk is divided into seven districts: Ipswich, Suffolk Coastal, Waveney, Mid Suffolk, Babergh, St Edmundsbury and Forest Heath.

SUFFOLK HUNDREDS

Historically, Suffolk was divided into two divisions, East and West, containing the following hundreds:

Eastern Division: Blything, Bosmere and Claydon, Carlford, Colners, Hoxne, Loes, Mutford and Lothinghland, Plomesgate, Samford, Thredling, Wangford, and Wilford.

Western Division: Babergh, Hartismere, Stow, Blackbourn, Cosford, Hartismere, Lackford, Risbridge, Stow, Thedwestry, and Thingoe.

THE RIVERS OF SUFFOLK

The River Alde has its source at Lawfield, near that of the River Blyth. It becomes tidal at the village of Snape and runs to the east of Aldeburgh, after which this part of the river takes its name.

The River Alde becomes known as the River Ore as it approaches Orford, where it once entered the sea. The mouth of the river is now a further 5 miles south.

The River Blythe has its source at Laxfield and a tidal estuary between Southwold and Walberswick. The Blyth Navigation canal was opened in 1761 and ran a total of 7 miles from Halesworth to the Blyth estuary. It became insolvent in 1884, was used occasionally until 1911 and was formally abandoned in 1934.

The River Deben rises in Debenham, runs through Woodbridge and turns into a tidal estuary before entering the North Sea at Felixstowe Ferry.

The River Dove is a tributary of the River Waveney, which starts at Horham and runs through the market town of Eye to the Waveney.

The River Gipping rises near Mendlesham Green and flows through Stowmarket, Needham Market and on to Ipswich, where it becomes the River Orwell. The old Ipswich and Stowmarket Navigation canal, opened in 1793, was achieved by the construction of some fifteen locks. It closed in 1922.

The River Kennett rises to the south of Dalham, flows through Moulton and Kennett, and joins Lee Brook, a tributary of the River Lark, south of Freckenham. The River Kennett usually runs dry in the summertime.

The River Lark is a tributary of the River Great Ouse. It rises at Bradfield Combust near Bury St Edmunds and flows through Bury, Mildenhall and across the Cambridgeshire border into Prickwillow and on to join the River Great Ouse south of Littleport.

The Little Ouse is a tributary of the River Great Ouse, and rises near Thelnetham and flows through Rushford, Thetford, Brandon and Hockwold before it joins the Great Ouse north of Littleport. The Little Ouse is also used to delineate part of the border between Norfolk and Suffolk.

The Minsmere river is formed out of the River Yox at Yoxford and flows through Middleton, Eastbridge and on to the Minsmere New Cut (built in 1812) and reaches the sea at Minsmere Sluice.

The Butley river, otherwise known as Butley Creek, has its source in Rendlesham Forest and is tidal from its confluence with the Ore at Boyton, and goes as far inland as Butley Mills and Butley village. The Butley Ferry, run by the volunteer ferrymen of the Alde & Ore Association, crosses the Butley Creek river and provides a link for pedestrians and cyclists between Orford, Boyton and Butley between Easter Saturday and September every year.

The River Ore is the name given to the final section of the River Alde from just above Orford until it joins the sea. It has one tributary, the Butley river, and Havergate Island is to be found at their confluence.

Oulton Dyke is about one mile long and connects Outon Broad to the River Waveney.

The River Waveney has its source near Redgrave and flows through Hoxne, Needham, Weybread, Homersfield, Earsham and Bungay, Beccles, Soerleton and over the border into Norfolk, where it flows through Haddiscoe, Breydon Water and out into the North Sea at Great Yarmouth.

The River Rat has its source at the village of Rattlesden and is the major tributary of the River Gipping.

The River Brett has its source near Lavenham. It flows through Hadleigh, Monks Eleigh, Brent Eleigh and Chelsworth to its confluence with the River Stour.

The River Orwell has the River Gipping, above the tidal limit at Stoke Bridge, as its source river. The Orwell broadens into an estuary at Ipswich, joins the River Stour at Shotley and flows into the North Sea at Felixstowe.

The River Stour rises in Eastern Cambridgeshire, flows east of Haverhill and through Cavendish, Bures, Sudbury, Nayland, Stratford St Mary and Dedham Vale. The Stour becomes tidal just before Manningtree and joins the North Sea at Harwich. It also forms most of the county boundary of Suffolk and Essex.

Stour Brook begins to the west of Haverhill and soon joins the River Stour near Wixoe, Essex.

The River Yox flows from the west of Peasenhall through Sibton and Yoxford, where it becomes the Minsmere river.

The Lark and the Little Ouse are the only notable Suffolk rivers that do not flow directly to the sea.

THE LOST TOWN OF DUNWICH

Through the years, the erosion of the county's soft cliffs and encroachments by the sea along the East Coast have caused the loss of hundreds of acres of land, and a number of settlements, including Covehithe, Pakefield, Aldeburgh and Slaughden, have all suffered from the loss. The hamlet of Newton has completely disappeared, but the most famous and important of all was the loss of the flourishing port town of Dunwich.

The decline of Dunwich began in 1328, when a tempest hit the coast and the hurricane-force winds drove the sea against the spit of land known as the King's Holme and pushed it into the harbour area, effectively rendering it impassable. All trade and revenues simply moved to Walberswick and left Dunwich to rot. Four hundred houses, along with shops, barns, windmills and two churches, St Martin and St Leonard, fell in the maelstrom. By the early twentieth century, all of the other churches and chapels eventually succumbed to the sea, as did most of the town. Despite the decline of the town they still maintained the ancient right to return two Members of Parliament. By the time of the 1832 Reform Act, there were only eight residents left in the constituency!

THORPENESS

The village of Thorpeness was a sleepy fishing hamlet until wealthy Scottish barrister G. Stuart Ogilvie bought the area and built a private fantasy holiday village in mock Tudor and Jacobean styles, where he invited friends and colleagues to stay during the summer months. He even created a shallow boating lake he called the Meare, with several coves and landings marked with names on a Peter Pan theme (author J.M. Barrie was a personal friend of Ogilvie and his family). Little islands on the Meare also contain locations inspired by the novel, such as Wendy's home, the pirates' lair and many others, where children are encouraged to play. The old crocodile still lurks around the place too! The outstanding feature of this dreamland of Thorpeness is its water tower, disguised as a five-storey clapboard house with imitation windows and a pitched roof 60ft up in the air. Ogilvie named it 'The Home of Peter Pan', but tenant Mrs Malcolm Mason loved it so much she was inspired to write the poem 'The House in the Clouds', and the name stuck.

SOME OF THE LESSER KNOWN MUSEUMS AND HISTORIC SITES OF SUFFOLK

Bawdsey Manor RADAR Transmitter Block, Bawdsey
Bentwaters Cold War Museum, Woodbridge
British Resistance Organisation Museum, Parham Airfield
Centre for Computing History, Haverhill
Clifford Road Air-Raid Shelter, Ipswich
Felixstowe Museum in the old Submarine Mining Establishment
    near Landguard Fort
Greene King Brewery Museum, Bury St Edmunds
HMS *Ganges* Museum, Shotley Marina, Shotley
Laxfield & District Museum, the Guildhall, Laxfield
Long Shop Museum, at the old works of Richard Garrett &
    Sons engineers
Lowestoft and East Suffolk Maritime Museum, Sparrow's Nest
    Gardens, Lowestoft
Lowestoft War Memorial Museum, Sparrow's Nest Gardens, Lowestoft
Martlesham Heath Control Tower Museum
Mechanical Music Museum, Cotton
Mincarlo, sidewinder fishing trawler museum ship, Lowestoft
Museum of Knots and Sailors' Ropework, Ipswich
Packhorse Bridge, Moulton
Royal Naval Patrol Service Museum, Lowestoft, Sparrow's Nest
    Gardens, Lowestoft
Ruins of Leiston Abbey (founded 1182)
Southwold Sailors' Reading Room, East Cliff, Southwold
St James' Chapel (built about 1250), Lindsey

Suffolk Underwater Studies Museum, Orford
Suffolk Heavy Horse Museum, Shire Hall, Woodbridge
The Amber Museum, Southwold
The ruins of the great church at Covehithe
Woodbridge Museum, Woodbridge

THE HEIGHTS OF IPSWICH

In 1930, the highest structures of Ipswich were recorded as:

St Mary's Church tower	176ft
Ipswich Electric shaft	176ft
St Peter's Church tower	93ft
St Lawrence's Church tower	90ft
Spring Road Viaduct	61ft

SUFFOLK LIGHTHOUSES

Lowestoft (High), current
structure built 1874, station
established in 1609. A white
flash every fifteen seconds.
Lowestoft North Pier, built
1847. Green light: four
seconds on, one second off.
Lowestoft South Pier,
built 1847. Red light: four
seconds on, one second off.
Pakefield, built 1832.
Inactive since 1864.
Southwold, built 1890. Four
flashes every twenty seconds,
white or red depending on
direction.

Landguard Point, established in 1848. Light house built in 1861.
Destroyed by fire in 1925.
Orfordness (High), current structure built in 1793. Station established in
1637. A white flash every five seconds.
Orfordness (Low), established in 1836. Lost to beach erosion in 1887.

THE MAGPIE GALLOWS SIGN

The present version of the unusual pub sign for the Magpie pub at Little Stonham, which straddles the Norwich-Ipswich turnpike (now the A140), was designed for Tollemache's Breweries by Messrs Cautley and Barefoot, architects in about 1931. A magpie was also kept in a cage by the pub door as a living sign for the pub. A gallows sign existed before this one, consisting of three or four small casks slung by a chain from the crossbeam. The casks were not of the usual barrel shape but the long cylindrical type of brandy cask.

CASTLES IN SUFFOLK

Bungay Castle: A Norman castle built by Roger Bigod around 1100, enlarged and improved, including the addition of the impressive gate towers by Roger Bigod, 5th Earl of Norfolk, in the thirteenth century.

Landguard Fort: Sited at Felixstowe, the fort is one of England's best preserved coastal defences, with a history that dates back almost 450 years.

Clare Castle: Originally a motte-and-bailey castle built by Richard Fitz Gilbert in the eleventh century, it was improved in stone during the thirteenth century.

Denham Castle: A motte-and-bailey fortification built in the twelfth century. Only some of its earthworks are visible today.

Eye Castle: Originally built by William Malet shortly after the Norman Conquest. Malet died while fighting Hereward the Wake in 1071. The castle was sacked and largely destroyed during the Second Baron's War in 1265.

Framlingham Castle: Originally built as a Norman motte-and-bailey, it was destroyed by Henry II after the revolt of 1173–74. The replacement, a structure of curtain wall and no keep, built by Roger Bigod, 2nd Earl of Norfolk and completed by 1213, is what can be seen today. Open to the public, it is well worth a visit.

Great Ashfield Castle: A medieval motte-and-bailey castle. Its few remains are overgrown.

Haughley Castle: With a base 210ft wide and 80ft tall, a motte-and-bailey castle built in the late eleventh century by Hugh de Montford. Besieged during the revolt of Henry's sons (1173–74), the castle was surrendered and burnt to the ground. The castle was not rebuilt after its destruction but most of its earthworks and motte may still be discerned.

Ipswich Castle: Built after the Norman Conquest, it was destroyed upon the orders of King Henry II after the revolt of his sons in 1173–74. The castle was not rebuilt, and nothing is known to remain of it today; even its location in the town is uncertain.

Lidgate Castle: Motte-and-bailey castle built about 1143 during a time of civil unrest, when King Stephen was keen to check any advances by rebel Baron Geoffrey de Mandeville into the region. The castle was abandoned about 1260 and has been largely destroyed through the development of the village and agriculture.

Mettingham Castle: Built under license in the fourteenth century by Sir John de Norwich as fortifications around his manor house. The castle was largely demolished in the eighteenth century.

Milden Castle: A twelfth-century motte-and-bailey castle. All that remains of it today is the earth mound upon which it was constructed.

Orford Castle: Built by Henry II between 1165 and 1173 to consolidate his royal power in the region. Its keep is of unique design (thought to be

based on Byzantine architecture), is well-preserved and was described by historian R. Allen Brown as 'one of the most remarkable keeps in England'.

Wingfield Castle: Built as a fortification, under license, for the manor house of Michael de la Pole, 1st Earl of Suffolk in the fourteenth century. Many of the old fortifications were extant up to the early twentieth century, when the north and south walls were demolished.

TREASURES OF THE ANCIENTS ... ON YOUR DOORSTEP!

The Anglo-Saxon cemetery containing the outstanding ship burial for a king, complete with all his grave goods, was excavated by self-taught Suffolk archaeologist Basil Brown at Sutton Hoo in 1939. The helmet that has become the undoubted icon of the Sutton Hoo burial along with his sword, heavily decorated buckles, shoulder clasps, bowls and plate form one of the greatest treasures of the British Museum.

The Hoxne Hoard, discovered by metal detector enthusiast Eric Lawes in November 1992, is the largest hoard of late Roman silver and gold discovered in Britain and the largest collection of gold and silver coins from the fourth and fifth centuries to be discovered anywhere in the Roman Empire. In November 1993, the Treasure Trove Reviewing Committee valued the hoard at £1.75 million, which was paid to Lawes, as finder of the treasure. He shared his reward with Peter Whatling, the farmer of the land where it was found.

There are two significant Ipswich Hoards. The first was a hoard of Anglo-Saxon silver coins from the reign of Aethelred the Unready (around 969–1016), discovered about 10ft under the doorstep of a house at the corner of Old Buttermarket and White Hart Lane in 1863. The second hoard consisted of a total of six Iron Age gold torcs (dated to around 75 BC), the first five of which were discovered in 1968 by the operator of a mechanical digger preparing the ground for a new housing estate at Belstead. The sixth torc, of a slightly different design, was found by one of the owners of the newly completed houses in 1969, when he was sorting through a pile of earth in his garden.

Rendham schoolboys Arthur Godbold and Arthur Baxter spotted what they thought was a football submerged in the waters of the River Alde in 1907. Retrieving the item from the waters, it turned out to be a life-size bronze head. The boys kept the item as a curiosity until it was spotted by a Benhall schoolmaster who believed it to be an antiquity, and purchased it from Godbold for 5s. Experts at the British Museum confirmed the schoolmaster's suspicions; it was, in fact, a bronze head wrenched from a life-size bronze statue of the Roman emperor Claudius (reigned AD 41–54) and was acquired for the museum for £15,500 in 1965. Copies of the head are on display at Ipswich Museum and in St Michael's Church in Rendham. It has been suggested the head came to be where it was found because it had been taken as a trophy from Camulodunum (Colchester) during Queen Boudicca's revolt in AD 60 and thrown into the river as part of a Celtic depository ritual.

The Mildenhall Treasure, a major hoard of highly decorated Roman silver tableware bowls and dishes dating from the fourth century, was unearthed by Gordon Butcher while he was ploughing a field at West Row, near Mildenhall, in 1942.

Snape Anglo-Saxon cemetery, consisting of nine or possibly ten tumuli has been subject to study and excavations since 1827. Among the finds here was a high-status ship burial by the Septimus Davision excavation in 1862 and, from 1867, a claw beaker and the Snape Ring, now housed in the British Museum.

The Wickham Market Hoard of 840 Iron-Age gold staters dating from 40 BC to AD 15 was found in a field at Dallinghoo by metal detector enthusiast Michael Dark in March 2008. The hoard was purchased by Ipswich Museum for £316,000 in June 2011.

The Brantham Hoard, consisting of ninety coins dating from the reign of Edward the Elder and buried in around AD 920–24, was discovered in 2003. They have subsequently been acquired by the Fitzwilliam Museum, Cambridge.

A Roman villa at Castle Hill, Ipswich, first recorded in the 1850s and first excavated in in 1931, provided extensive finds including samian pottery, iron household tools, personal accessories such as tweezers and finger rings, and a jet plaque depicting ancient Roman king Atys, as well as mosaics.

A superb golden plaque, finely engraved and inlaid with black niello bearing the Latin inscription *scs evangelista ioannis* (St John the Baptist) and the symbol of John the Evangelist, was found by a fisherman in the River Ouse at Brandon in 1978.

A 900-year-old pendant in the form of a cross made from silver and originally gilded, engraved with an image of Christ on a cross and thought to have contained a religious relic, was discovered at Thwaite in 1999. Believed to have belonged to an abbot or nobleman, it is now known as The Thwaite Cross and is one of the treasures of the British Museum.

THE MUNICIPALITY OF IPSWICH

The Charter of James II confirmed the privileges of Ipswich in 1688 to have a municipality consisting of two bailiffs, a high steward, a recorder, twelve portmen (four of whom were justices of the peace), twenty-four chief constables (two of whom were coroners), twelve senior head-boroughs, a town clerk, treasurer, two chamberlains, a water bailiff, four sergeants-at-mace, two bailiffs who also acted as port admirals, claiming all waifs, strays and goods cast on the shore in their jurisdiction, which extended to the sea below Harwich and Landguard Fort. This constituted the governing body of the town until the passing of the Municipal Corporations Act of 1835, which divided the town into five wards and vested the government of the town with a mayor, recorder, high steward, a Bench of twenty magistrates, ten aldermen and thirty common councilmen.

SOME OF THE PRINCIPAL SEATS OF SUFFOLK AND THEIR OCCUPANTS IN 1929

Ashe High House, Viscount Ullswater
Barton Mere, Brigadier General Morey Quayle Jones
Bawdsey Manor, Sir William Eley Cuthbert Quilter
Blackheath, Captain Frederick Charles Ulick Vernon-Wentworth
Boxted Hall, John George Weller-Poley
Brandeston Hall, Carron Scrimgeour
Brettenham Park, Sir Thomas Courtenay Theydon Warner
Chediston Park, Eugene F.L. Leguen de Lacroix
Glemham Hall, Captain John Murray Cobbold
The Grove, Walsham-le-Willows, Captain Stewart le Poer Trench
Lackfield Manor House, Reverend John Shuttleworth Holden
Lanwades Hall, Moulton, Herbert Sidebottom
Little Thurlow Hall, Hugh Raincock le Fleming
Rockalls Hall, Polstead, Murdock Mackenzie Hodson Mackenzie
Stoke Priory, Henry Lewis Dillman Engleheart

Theberton House, Louis E. Meinertzhagen
Tostock Place, Reverend The Honourable Luis Chandos Francis Temple Morgan-Grenville (Master of Kinloss)
Woodbridge Abbey, Colonel Ranulphus John Carthew

TWENTY LOST
COUNTRY HOUSES OF SUFFOLK

Acton Place
Assington Hall
Barham Hall
Carlton Hall
Drinkstsone Hall
Flixton Hall
Gipping Hall
Hobland Hall
Holton Hall
Hunston Hall

Kenton Hall
Little Saxham Hall
Livermere Hall
Oakley Park
Ousden Hall
Rendlesham Hall
Rushbrook Hall
Sudbourne Hall
Thornham Park
Wrentham Hall

THE POPULATION OF SUFFOLK

(According to the Office of National Statistics)

1801	210,431	1911	394, 060
1811	234,211	1921	400,058
1821	270,542	1931	401,114
1831	296,317	1951	442,561
1841	315,073	1961	471,974
1851	337,215	1971	546,194
1861	337,070	1981	590,133
1871	348,869	1991	636,266
1881	356,893	2001	668,553
1891	374,781	2011	728,200
1901	373,353		

LAST OF THE POST MILLS

Post mills were once the most common and characteristic of all windmills in Suffolk; indeed most villages and every town would once have had at least one windmill within its bounds.

Some fine examples have been preserved such as those at Thorpeness, Holton, Webster's Mill at Framsden, Saxtead Green Mill at Framlingham and Upthorpe Mill at Stanton, but most have been lost down the years.

In 1937, the Suffolk Preservation Society carried out a survey of post mills in Suffolk that still had significant remaining structure and features, such as intact sails, which was published listing the following. If they are no longer extant and their fate is known it has been added in brackets:

Drinkstone
Earl Soham (Demolished 1947)
Earl Soham, Clowes Corner (Demolished 1947)
Eye (Blown down 1955)
Framlingham, Saxtead Green
Framsden
Friston
Gedding (Demolished 1944)
Halesworth, Calver's Mill (Demolished 1942)
Hartest (Burned down *c.* 1958)
Holton St Peter
Laxfield (Demolished *c.* 1941)
Parham (Demolished 1944)
Peasenhall (Demolished *c.* 1957)
Petthaugh (Demolished 1957)
South Elmham, St Michael (Demolished *c.* 1955)
Stanningfield
Stanton, Upthorpe Mill
Stradbroke, Skinner's Mill (Demolished *c.* 1941)
Stradbroke, Barley Green (Demolished 1941)
Swilland (Demolished *c.* 1953)
Syleham (Blown down 1987)
Thornham Magna (Burned down 1959)
Thorpeness
Thurston (Demolished *c.* 1953)
Wenhaston, Kitty Mill (Demolished *c.* 1967)
Westhall, Mill Common (Demolished 1957)
Westleton (Demolished 1963)
Wetheringsett, Broad Green Mill (Demolished 1957)
Woolpit (Collapsed 1963)
Worlingworth (Demolished 1952)
Wrentham, Carter's Mill (Demolished 1955)

SOME OF THE LESSER KNOWN OR MORE UNUSUAL LISTED BUILDINGS AND STRUCTURES

Grade I
The Willis Faber and Dumas Insurance headquarters building in Ipswich, designed by Norman Foster and built 1970–75.

Grade II
The K6 telephone kiosks at Stanningfield, Earl Soham and Orford
The Cowshed Laundry and Dairy Range at Easton Farm Park
The milestone, 10m south of Yoxholme
Denes High School, Yarmouth Road, Lowestoft
Needham Market railway station
Hand Pump and Timber Casing and Warners Almshouses, Boyton
The signpost near St Peter's Church, Yoxford
The pillar box at the east end of Double Street, Framlingham
The eighteenth-century Gate Pier to the south of Parham House
The Sick House, Grundisburgh Road, Woodbridge
The Elephant & Castle public house, Hospital Road, Bury St Edmunds
The Pillar of Salt road sign on Angel Hill, Bury St Edmunds
   (designed by Basil Oliver, Town Council architect in 1935)
The garden wall to Regency House Hotel, Looms Lane, Bury St Edmunds
The pump in front of the Mills Almshouses, Framlingham
The water tower, Nacton
Gateway, balustrading and steps over the Ha Ha, near Orwell Park School
The post office, The Street, Walpole
The kitchen store in the garden at Heveningham Hall

TEN PLACE NAMES YOU DON'T EXPECT TO FIND IN SUFFOLK

America Hill (Witnesham)
Gibraltar (near Ashbocking)
California (Wickham Market)
The Trossachs (Oulton Broad)
Klondyke (Bury St Edmunds)
Mendip Road (Lowestoft)
Dublin (near Thorndon)
New England Lane (near Newmarket)
Hyde Park Corner (Ipswich)

Nova Scotia Lane (Brent Eleigh)
Pitcairn Road (Ipswich)
Waterloo Avenue (Leiston)
Edinburgh Gardens (Claydon)
Little London Hill (Stowmarket)
Swiss Farm (Ipswich)
Novocastria (Waldringfield)
Sodom and Gomorrah (Higham)

ECCENTRIC SUFFOLK PLACE NAMES

Nuttery Vale (Cross Street)
Nonsuch Meadows (Sudbury)
The Devil's Handbasin (Brome)
Flempton
Rat Hill (Harkstead)
Great Tufts (Capel St Mary)
Rattlerow Hill (Stradbroke)
Finger Bread Hill (Trimley St Martin)
The Grindle (Burstall)
Grundisburgh
Hill of Health (Brockley Corner)
Red Sleeve (Capel St Mary)
Amos's Skirts (Benacre)
Helions Bumpstead
Uggeshall
Pixey Green (Stradbroke)
Dandy Corner (Cotton)
Beggar's Bush (Gazeley)
Sweffling
Wherstead Ooze
The Spong (Metfield)
Sprites End (Trimley St Mary)
Nedging Tye
Wigwam Hill (Magpie Green)
Brimstone Covert (Frostenden)
Thingoe Hill (Bury St Edmunds)
Burnthouse Queach (Harkstead)
Puddingpokes (Hemley)

AND SOME ECCENTRIC STREET NAMES

Bent Lane (Rushmere
   St Andrew)
Swine's Green (Beccles)
Clench Close (Ipswich)
One Eyed Lane (Weybread)
Pesthouse Lane (Barham)
Gobbets Lane (Hinderclay)
Plash Road (Bedingfield)
Great Whip Street (Ipswich)
Wacker Field Road

(Rendlesham)
Grub Lane (Ilketshall St Lawrence)
Scuffin's Lane (Cotton)
Swilltub Lane (Cotton)
World's End Lane (Buxhall)
Slushy Lane (Lower Holbrook)
Slugs Lane (Somerleyton)
Shoe Devil Lane
   (Ilketshall St Margaret)
Wriggle Street (Brandeston)

SUFFOLK PLACE NAMES
TO MAKE YOU THINK TWICE

Fiddler's Lane (Eye)
Wangford
Burnt Dick Hill (Boxted)
Westley Bottom
Wadd Lane (Gromford)
Rogue's Lane (Wickham Market)
Bloodman's Corner (Hopton on Sea)
Smear Marshes (Cove Bottom)
Pratt's Shrubbery (Woolverstone)
Puttock End (Semer)
Thieves Lane (Grimstone End)
Deadman's Lane (Stoke Ash)
Reydon Smear
Earth Holes Wood (Thorington)

Upend
Fingery Grove (Bentley)
Screw Park (Redisham)
Balls Hill (Hitcham)
Piper's Went (Raydon)
Shaker's Road (Wangford)
Frizzler's Green (Great Saxham)
Cock's Head (Hargrave)
Pokerage Corner (Thurston)
Cock and End (Stradishall)
Cock Lane (Hundon)
Bushey Hole (Capel St Andrew)
Lump Pits Hole (Hoxne)

NATURAL HISTORY – SPECIAL TO SUFFOLK

The Suffolk Wasp (*Dyscritulus suffolciensis*)
was discovered in the county by entomologist
Claude Morley (1874–1951).

A population of the rare Scarce Emerald Damselfly
(*Lestes dryas*), believed to have become extinct in the
1980s, was discovered at Market Weston Fen in 2007.

The Pied Avocet (*Recurvirostra avosetta*) became extinct in Britain in 1840 but had a successful re-colonisation at Minsmere in 1947.

The Sizewell Bunting bird, a hybrid between the Pine Bunting and the Yellowhammer, was recorded in the county in 1982.

A black widow (*Latrodectus*) spider, one of the world's most deadly arachnids, was discovered in Martlesham Heath when a container from Singapore was opened at a road haulage firm in Beardmore Park in 2010.

The Frölichi (*Haploharpalus*) beetle was a unique discovery made in Suffolk in 1897. In 1898, over eighty of them were recorded upon Foxhall Plateau but all trace of the insect had disappeared again by 1900.

Beccles and the surrounding district suffered a plague of the Antler Moth (*Cerapteryx graminis*) in July 1937.

In September 2004, the moth species *Catocala conjuncta* (which was previously unrecorded in Britain) was found at Minsmere and given the common name of the Minsmere Crimson Underwing.

The only place the Great Raft Spider (*Dolomedes fimbriatus*) may be found in the British Isles is at Redgrave and Lopham Fen.

Common Cranes (*Grus grus*), common to East Anglia until about 1600, have nested almost annually in Suffolk since 1983.

LOST AND FOUND FUNGI

The pepperpot earthstar (*Myriostoma coliforme*) fungi, described as a new species in 1776, is found in roadside banks and hedgerows amongst nettles in Suffolk and Norfolk. It was also recorded in Kent, Middlesex, and Worcestershire during the first half of the nineteenth century, but by 1880 it was believed to have disappeared, until a specimen was found at the edge of an oak woodland near Ipswich in 2006.

BREEDS OF BATS FOUND IN SUFFOLK

Lesser Horseshoes (*Rhinolophus hipposideros*)
Barbastelle (*Barbastella barbastellus*)

Brown Long-eared (*Plecotus auritus*)
Daubentons (*Myotis daubentonii*)
Leislers (*Nyctalus leisleri*)
Natterers (*Myotis nattereri*)
Noctule (*Nyctalus noctula*)
Pipistrelle (*Pipistrellus pipistrellus*)
Serotine (*Eptesicus serotinus*)
Whiskered (*Myotis mystacinus*)

BRAMFIELD OAK

The old Bramfield Oak that stood in the grounds of Bramfield Hall was claimed to have been 'a giant' in the days of Thomas Becket. It stood as a far-seen landmark for centuries afterwards until it fell in June 1843, leaving just a stump.

MARCHING SPIDERS

The middle of Broad Street in Bury St Edmunds was infested by thousands of spiders of a reddish colour in September 1660. Spectators judged them to be as many as would fill a peck. Apparently, marching together in a strange kind of order, they made their way to a Mr Duncomb's house. Many of them got under the door and spun a huge web between the door posts. Wrapping themselves in the web, they made two great parcels which dangled towards the ground. The servants in the house noticed this, fetched some dry straw and laid it under each parcel. Putting fire to it, a sudden flame consumed the majority of them. Mr Duncomb, 'a member of the late parliament', believed the spiders were sent to his house by witches.

NATIONAL NATURE RESERVES

There are eight National Nature Reserves in Suffolk, they are:

Benacre (part of the Broads National Park)
Bradfield Woods
Cavenham Heath
Orfordness-Havergate

Redgrave and Lopham Fen
Thetford Heath
Walberwick Nature Reserve
Westleton Heath

TWENTY SITES OF SPECIAL SCIENTIFIC INTEREST IN SUFFOLK

All of the following places, be they large or small, are chosen to be designated SSSIs by Natural England because of their fauna, flora, geological or physical features:

Arger Fen	122.8 acres
Black Ditches, Cavenham	2.8 acres
Bobbitshole, Belstead	4.2 acres
Bugg's Hole Fen, Thelnetham	9.6 acres
Crag Pit, Sutton	1.8 acres
Fox Fritillary Meadow, Framsden	6.0 acres
Hopton Fen	37.8 acres
Horringer Court Caves	9.5 acres
Knettishall Heath	226.4 acres
Lakenheath Warren	1,453.2 acres
Milden Thicks	104.5 acres
Minsmere (Walberswick Heaths and Marshes)	5,747.7 acres
Newbourn Springs	38.8 acres
Orwell Estuary	3,298.8 acres
Round Hill Pit, Aldeburgh	1.2 acres
Stour Estuary	5,552.6 acres
The Glen Chalk Caves, Bury St Edmunds	4.0 acres
Trundley and Wadgell's Wood, Great Thurlow	196.1 acres
Waldringfield Pit	0.2 acres
Wortham Ling	131.5 acres

UNCOMMON WINTER VISITOR AND PASSAGE MIGRANT BIRDS OF SUFFOLK

Bean Goose (*Anser fabalis*)
Black Throated Diver (*Gavia arctica*)
Black-Necked Grebe (*Podiceps nigricollis*)
Bohemian Waxwing (*Bombycilla garrulous*)
European Shag (*Phalacrocorax aristotelis*)
Horned (Shore) Lark (*Eremophila alpestris*)
Lapland Longspur (*Calcarius lapponicus*)
Little Auk (*Alle alle*)
Merlin (*Falco columbarius*)
Red-Crested Pochard (*Netta rufina*)
Red Kite (*Milvus milvus*)

Rough-Legged Buzzard (*Buteo lagopus*)
Velvet Scoter (*Melanitta fusca*)
Razorbill (*Alca torda*)
Water Pipit (*Anthus spinoletta*)
Whooper Swan (*Cygnus cygnus*)

GREAT BUSTARD

The Great Bustard (*Otis tarda*) was once a familiar native bird in Britain, but its major downfall was that it was a very tasty game bird with plenty of meat on it – some male specimens can stand over a metre tall and one of the largest ever caught weighed in at a massive 21kg. It was recorded as having a taste like something between pheasant and turkey that made it a highly popular dish on British dinner tables, and as they became more and more scarce, could command greater prices. One of the last bastions for 'droves' of Great Bustard was Newmarket Heath, but they were hunted there too; indeed, one large male bird was surprised by a dog there in 1819, was taken to Leadenhall Market in London and sold for five guineas. Eventually, the colony on Newmarket Heath was wiped out and the poor bird was finally hunted to extinction in the United Kingdom in the 1830s. Great Bustards are still prevalent in other parts of the world, such as the Middle East, Greece, France, Germany and Russia, and attempts have and continue to be made to reintroduce the Great Bustard to Britain.

SOME OF THE
RARE BUTTERFLIES OF SUFFOLK

Clouded Yellow (*Colias croceus*)
Dingy Skipper (*Erynnis tages*)
Purple Emperor (*Apatura Iris*)
Silver-studded Blue (*Plebejus argus*)
Silver-washed Fritillary (*Argynnis paphia*)
Swallowtail (*Papilo machaon*)
White-letter Hairstreak
  (*Strymonidia w-album*)
White Admiral (*Limenitis camilla*)

ALL CREATURES...

Suffolk names for creatures great and small:

Arrawiggle – ear wig
Barley Bird – nightingale
Badgett – badger
Bishy-barnibee – ladybird
Blood-alp – Bullfinch
Billy-witch, Butter-witch or cock-hornybug – cockchafer
Bor or buh – term of familiar address
Cannock-Crow – a grey crow that was believed to 'come from the
    north in bad weather'
Cavve – calf
Come-Backs – guinea fowl
Develin – a swift
Dicky – donkey
Dodaman or Hodmadod – snail
Dow-felfet – a large thrush with variegated breast
Dow – dove
Flitter-mouse – a bat
Fulfer – fieldfare
Harnsie – heron
Hayjack – willow warbler
Hedge-grubber – sparrow
Hobgoblin – turkey cock
Horn-pie – lapwing
Jacob – a large toad
Jinny-reen – wren
King Harry – goldfinch
Miller-moth – a large, white moth
Minefer – stoat
Pick-cheese – titmouse
Pot-ladles – tadpoles
Pudding-poke – long-tailed tit
Rig – a badly castrated ram
Southwold crow – seagulls
Spink – chaffinch
Titter-reen – gold-crested wren

SOME SUFFOLK NAMES FOR FLOWERS, SEEDS AND BERRIES

A-kiss-behind-the-garden-gate – Pansy
Bear's Eyes – Poltanthus
Bread and Cheese – Mallow
Brushes and Combs – Wild Teasel
Bull Daisies – Ox Eye
Fiddle-sticks – Water Figwort
Goslings – Palm Blossom
Grandfather Greybeard – Wild Clematis
Gypsy Rhubarb – Burdock
Haste to the Wedding – Rock Cress
Huntsman's Cap or Hogknife – Iris
Jack-at-the-Garden-Gate – Heartsease
Jam Tarts – Willow Herb
John-go-to-bed-at-noon – Goat's Beard
King Cups – Marsh Marigold
Lady's Bonnets – Dove Flower
Lady's Frock – Cardamine
Lady's Hair – Quaking Grass
Lamb's Tails – Hazel Catkins
Mary Buds or Gold Cups – Buttercup
Milkmaids – Meadow Bitter Cress
Nathan-driving-his-chariot – Monkshood
New Year's Gift – Winter Aconite
Nipnoses – Snapdragon
Pig's Tootles – Bird's Foot
Queen Anne's Needlework – London Pride
Ready Money or Miser's Shillings – Honesty
Shepherd's Weatherglass – Scarlet Pimpernel
Shirt Buttons – Stitchwort
Snakes – Campion
Sweet Betsy – London Pride
Sweethearts – Cleavers
Time Tables or What O'Clock – Seed heads of Dandelion

2

THE MILITARY, BATTLES AND WAR

DISTANT DRUMS

The Battle of Bury St Edmunds on 17 October 1173 was actually fought in the nearby village of Fornham All Saints. Robert Whitehands, Earl of Leicester had raised an army of 3,000 Flemings against Henry II in sympathy for his royal sons. After landing at Walton Whitehands, his troops marched to Framlingham Castle where they were welcomed by Hugh Bigod. Mustering more troops and fortified by the sacking of Haughley Castle, they marched on to Bury. They were met at Fornham by the King's forces, soldiers who were bloodied and victorious over the Scots, led by Humphrey de Boun, surprising Whitehands' troops at Fornham and forcing them back to Fornham St Genevieve. Whitehands' entire force was either killed or taken prisoner after a brave final stand in the church. The bones of about forty of the soldiers were discovered lying head-to-head in a mound near the church in the eighteenth century.

SUFFOLK HEARTS OF OAK

In 1338 a fleet of Suffolk ships assembled at Goseford (the old name for Bawdsey Haven) and joined an expedition from the Humber to Antwerp.

In 1340 a fleet of 250 ships sailed from Orwell and gained a decisive victory over the French fleet at Sluys.

In 1346, Edward III mustered a fleet of 700 ships to attack Calais; of these Suffolk sent 48 ships and 989 men – specifically, as written in historical record:

Donwich, 6 ships
Orford, 3 ships
Goford, 13 ships
Herwich, 14 ships
Ipswich, 12 ships

PEASANTS REVOLT

The Peasants Revolt led by John Wrawe broke out at Liston on 12 June 1381. By the evening, the rebels were at the gates of Bury issuing a proclamation demanding support from the population on pain of decapitation. On 14 June, they attacked the abbey, captured and beheaded Sir John Cavendish, the Lord Chief Justice, and later went on to do the same to the Prior of Mildenhall, bringing his head back on a pole for all to see and deride at Bury. Henry Despencer, the warlike Bishop of Norwich, was soon despatched with his troops and mercenaries and put down the rebels in a bloody battle.

IPSWICH TO ARMS!

Bacon's *Annalls of Ipswiche* records the town ordnance of 11 October 1452, whereby:

Every man within the liberty of this Towne resident, before Munday next, viz. All having shopps, shall kepe one good staffe: and every servant of lawful age shall have one staff in their shopps or houses under penalty of 4d. To wait uppon the Bayliffs when necessity shall be, by day or by night, ffor the good and honour of the Towne. And that other inhabitants of greater ability in the same Towne shall have Jacks, Sallets, Bowes, arrives, swords, Targetts, Poleaxes and other weapons of warre ready at an hower to defend themselves and withstand the enemies of the King and Kingdom as they ought.

BEATING THE ARMADA

When the Spanish Armada loomed in 1588, 2,500 Suffolk men were raised to garrison Tilbury Fort and 2,000 more were sent to defend Suffolk ports and landing places while the town of Ipswich furnished two ships, armed and manned at their own cost, and sent them to serve with the defending fleet.

CIVIL WAR STRIFE

The traditional Mayday celebrations were a popular holiday before the Civil War, and when it was abolished the people of Bury were not going to be ruled over without a fight. On 1 May 1648, about 600 people gathered together and raised a Maypole, proclaiming it was done 'For God and King Charles'. Raiding the local magazine and laying hold of sympathetic trained bands, the mob manned defensive positions across the town. News rapidly reached Sir Thomas Fairfax, who sent Colonel Whalley to quell the disturbance. After a brief fracas between scouting parties, where two townsfolk and two horses were killed, two MPs – Sir William Barnardiston and Sir William Playters, who had travelled down with Colonel Whalley – bravely approached

the rebels. They offered the rioters a chance to lay down their arms, submit themselves to parliament and restore the magazine they raided; they would be pardoned for their 'tumult'. The townsfolk took the easy and sensible option and laid down their arms in the Market House without incident.

THE BATTLE OF SOLE BAY

Fought on 28 May 1672, the battle is celebrated as an 'obstinate and sanguinary naval engagement', when the fleets of England and France were combined against the Dutch. England and France fielded 101 men-of-war ships, plus fire ships and tenders carrying a total of 6,018 guns and 34,500 men, whereas the Dutch came with 168 vessels, of which 91 were men-of-war. The English and French were laying upon the bay 'in negligent posture'. When one of the naval commanders, the Earl of Sandwich, informed his senior, HRH James, Duke of York, he was censured and his courage questioned in reply. When the Dutch ships approached, he was first out of the Bay; had Sandwich not acted promptly, de Ruyter's fire ships would have destroyed the combined fleets. This timely action enabled the ships of the Duke and the French to disentangle themselves, and bought them valuable time as Sandwich returned to do battle, determined 'to conquer or die'. Sandwich proved more than a match for the Dutch Admiral, who he engaged full-on and slew with his own hand, sinking a man-of-war and three other vessels. But sadly, the shot of the Dutch broadsides slowly decimated his crew and sunk Sandwich's ship. The battle raged on all day and the exchange of fire was declared by many old sea dogs to be unprecedented. Night-time saw the Dutch ships disengage and the English and French declared the victors. The losses on both sides were thought to have been nearly equal – the Battle of Sole Bay was a near-run thing!

THE BATTLE OF LOWESTOFT

When thinking of naval engagements in Suffolk, most think of the Battle of Sole Bay, but equally significant was the engagement off Lowestoft on 3 June 1665, fought between Charles II's English Fleet and the Dutch. The Dutch fleet consisted of 102 men-of-war,

17 yachts and fire ships while the English fleet comprised 114 men-of-war and 28 fire ships. In a battle which raged between three in the morning and seven in the evening, the Dutch ended up being completely routed with the loss of 18 ships captured and 14 sunk or burnt. The English lost only 1 ship and 250 men, and the wounded were said not to exceed 350.

THE LAST INVASION LANDING BY FOREIGN TROOPS IN ENGLAND

On 2 July 1667, the Dutch anchored about 50 sails to the East of Landguard, and landed 1,000 soldiers and 400 marines under the fire of the fleet on the beaches of Felixstowe. During the course of the day they approached Landguard Fort and attacked using scaling ladders, hand grenades and muskets. The Dutch attempted two assaults and were repulsed on both occasions, finally withdrawing in disorder. Out of the 500 soldiers at Landguard Fort, only one member of the garrison was killed and four wounded, including the Governor, Captain Nathaniel Darrell, who was hit in the shoulder by a musket ball.

YEOMANRY IN EVERY WAY

The Loyal Suffolk Yeomanry was formed by agricultural writer Arthur Young, of Bradfield Combust, in 1793.

PIRATES!

The late eighteenth century was a time when French and American privateers stalked the waters off Eastern England and even humble fishermen and their boats were in danger. A cod smack sailing off Southwold in 1780 was pursued by what they believed was a heavily armed smuggling vessel. They were saved when the pursuing ship was forced to flee when a fleet of colliers heaved into view. This aggressive smuggling ship transpired to be a 150-ton American privateer named *Fearnought*. Armed with eighteen 4-pounder cannons, the ship was under the command of notorious pirate Daniel Fall, who terrorised the East Coast until he was finally chased away by HMS *Albermarle* under the command of no lesser man than Horatio Nelson.

INVASION SIGNALS

The fears of invasion along our coast during the Napoleonic Wars resulted in a chain of signal stations being set up in high ground at Bawdsey, Orford, Felixstowe, Aldeburgh, Dunwich, Easton Cliff, Covehithe, Kessingland and Gunton, while Lowestoft and Woodbridge fixed tar barrels atop their church steeples which could be lit as an emergency signal in the event of a night landing. These, along with the erection of a telegraph on Rushmere steeple, gave a command of the coast from Aldeburgh to Harwich. These telegraphs worked on a semaphore principle, originally with six arms (later reduced to just two); this meant that a message could be relayed from Whitehall to any of these stations along the coast in less than an hour and vice versa.

MARTELLO TOWERS

Named after the round fortress, part of a larger Genovese defence system at Mortella Point in Corsica, the Martello Towers in Suffolk are part of a long chain of 103 towers that extended along the south and East Coast of England, from Seaford in Sussex to Aldeburgh, erected by the Board of Ordnance between 1804 and 1812 as fortifications to help repulse any attempted invasion by the forces of Napoleon. The eighteen Martello Towers in Suffolk are located at:

Shotley Gate
Near Shotley Marine
Walton Ferry (Demolished)
The tip of Langer Point (Swept away by the sea)
Felixstowe seafront
Felixstowe, Bulls Cliff
Felixstowe, near the old Bartlett Hospital
Felixstowe, also near the old Bartlett Hospital (Demolished)
Felixstowe Ferry
Felixstowe, River Deben
Bawdsey Manor (Destroyed)
Bawdsey Cliffs
Bawdsey beach (Dismantled)
Bawdsey
Alderton
Shingle Street
Near the mouth of the River Ore (Demolished)
Slaughden, near Aldeburgh

The largest and most northerly of the entire 'chain' of Martello Towers is located at Slaughten, near Aldeburgh. Built in a quatrefoil shape, 40ft high with a diameter of 77ft, this fortification had a stone-flagged battery on the roof with mountings for guns and a high parapet for shelter. Over a million bricks were used in its construction. Purchased in 1971 by the Landmark Trust, they have sensitively restored it and it is now available to rent for short breaks.

All other East Coast Martello Towers were cam-shaped, 33ft high with a diameter of 55ft. Each tower required 150 rods of 5,000 bricks (750,000 bricks).

TWELVE BITS ABOUT 'THE OLD DOZEN'

The origins of the Suffolk Regiment can be traced back to the Duke of Norfolk's Regiment of Foot, raised against the threatened Monmouth Rebellion in 1685.

Designated the 12th Foot Regiment in 1747, it was formally given the county title of the Suffolk Regiment under the Childers Reforms of the British Army in 1881, but their old Foot Regiment roots were remembered in the nickname of 'The Old Dozen'.

The regimental motto was '*Stabilis*'.

The cap badge of the Suffolk Regiment contains the Castle and Key of Gibraltar as its central device and the motto '*Montis Insignia Calpe*'. The badge of the Rock of Gibraltar was awarded to the regiment in recognition of their distinguished services breaking the Siege of Gibraltar in 1781.

The territorial battalions of the Suffolk Regiment wore a badge containing the two-turret castle of Bury St Edmunds, rather than the three-turret castle of Gibraltar, worn by all other battalions.

The 12th Regiment distinguished themselves at the Battle of Minden, fought on 1 August 1759. The regiments involved in the action had advanced through rose gardens to the battleground and decorated their tricorn hats and grenadier caps with these flowers. Minden Day was always remembered on the anniversary of the battle, and the Suffolk

Regiment wore red and yellow roses in their caps for the special parades on that day.

Up until 1858, the Regimental March of the Suffolk Regiment was 'The Duchess'. Other marches were tried for a while, but 'The Duchess' was reintroduced until 'Speed the Plough' was adopted by all battalions at the Regimental March, about 1898.

Two Suffolk Regiment soldiers have been awarded the Victoria Cross, namely Sergeant Arthur Frederick Saunders, 9th (Service) Battalion, for gallantry at Loos, France, on 26 September 1915, and Corporal Sidney James Day, 11th Service Battalion, for conspicuous gallantry at Hargicourt, France, on 26 August 1917.

Out of the 1,000 men of the 2nd Battalion, the Suffolk Regiment, 720 men were killed, wounded or taken prisoner during eight hours of fighting at the Battle of Le Cateau, France, on 26 August 1914.

A total of almost 7,000 officers and men lost their lives while serving in the Suffolk Regiment during the First World War.

The 7th Battalion, the Suffolk Regiment re-formed in May 1940, and were initially nicknamed 'The String and Cardboard Suffolks'. They converted to a regiment in the Royal Armoured Corps (142nd Regiment RAC) in 1941, and were the only battalion of the Suffolk Regiment entitled to wear black berets during the Second World War.

The Suffolk Regiment was amalgamated with the Royal Norfolk Regiment and 1st Battalion, the Cambridgeshire Regiment, to create the East Anglian Regiment in 1959. This regiment subsequently joined with a number of other regiments from Eastern England to create the Royal Anglian Regiment in 1964.

The regimental chapel of the Suffolk Regiment is to be found in St Mary's Church, Bury St Edmunds.

TRAFALGAR VETERAN

Captain Edward Rotheram (1753–1830), commander of HMS *Royal Sovereign* at the Battle of Trafalgar in 1805, retired to Bildeston and lies buried in the churchyard of St Mary Magdelene Church.

OLD GROG

Admiral Edward Vernon of Orwell Park (1684–1757), victor of the Battle of Portobello in 1739, was known to the sailors in the British Navy as 'Old Grog'. This nickname derived from the old grogram coat he unfailingly wore on the quarter-deck of his ships. His name also became attached to his policy of mixing water with the brandy or rum ration in his fleet. An unpopular policy in its day, the name stuck and even today glasses of 'grog' are raised with a wry smile by sailors past and present. He rests in Nacton Church.

THE BEARER OF BAD NEWS …
FOR NAPOLEON

Sir Henry Bunbury (1778–1860) had a fine military career during which he rose to the rank of Lieutenant-General. He distinguished himself during the Battle of Maida in 1806 and became the man who, while Under-Secretary of State for War and The Colonies (1809–1816), was responsible for informing Napoleon of his sentence of deportation to St Helena. Appointed High Sheriff of Suffolk in 1825, and MP for the county from 1830–32, Bunbury lived at Barton Hall and is buried at Great Barton.

SOME DISTINGUISHED SUFFOLK SAILORS

Admiral of the Fleet, Sir John Ashby (1646–1693), grew up in Suffolk and fought at in the Battle of Texel, and distinguished himself at the Battle of Beachy Head. His conduct received praise from Queen Mary, and Ashby was named joint Admiral of the Fleet with Sir Richard Haddock and Sir Henry Killigrew. He died at Portsmouth but his body was returned to Suffolk and he was buried at Lowestoft.

Vice Admiral James Mighells (1664–1733) distinguished himself at the Battle of Malaga in 1704, commanded an expedition off the coast of Spain in 1719, captured Vigo and brought back Spanish treasure worth in excess of £80,000, and was made Comptroller of the Navy. He was buried in Lowestoft Church.

Rear Admiral Richard Utber was born at Lowestoft; he distinguished himself in a number of actions against the Dutch fleet, notably at the Battle of Lowestoft (1665). In recognition of his bravery he was appointed Rear Admiral of the White Squadron in 1666 and went on to capture a number of French and Dutch ships worth considerable bounty. He died in 1669 and is commemorated in Lowestoft Church.

Captain John Utber, son of Rear Admiral Richard, also fought at the Battle of Lowestoft. He was killed in action at the attack on Bergan in 1665.

Sir Andrew Leake, son of a Lowestoft merchant, and who became known as 'Queen Anne's handsome captain', commanded the Torbay at the Battle of Vigo and was killed at the Battle of Malaga in 1704.

Captain Thomas Arnold (1679–1737) led the boarding party from the *Superbe* when the *Royal San Philip* was captured, and his son, Midshipman Thomas Arnold, accompanied Lord Anson round the world aboard the *Centurion* (1740–44).

Admiral Pelham Aldrich (1844–1930) was born at Mildenhall and entered the Royal Navy as a cadet in 1859. He was part of the Challenger Scientific Expedition (1872–76), which made a number of important discoveries that laid the foundations for the subject of oceanography. Exploration became his life in the Royal Navy. In 1875 he commanded the Western Sledge Party to Ellesmere Island, in North America and Cape Aldrich was named in his honour. Moreover, Mount Aldrich in Antarctica was named after Aldrich by Robert Scott in recognition of his assistance in the preparations for Scott's expedition. Aldrich was promoted to Admiral in 1907. He retired from the Royal Navy the following year and moved to Great Bealings, where he lived out the rest of his days and is buried in the churchyard.

Vice Admiral Robert FitzRoy (1805–1865) was born at Ampton Hall, Ampton, and was a pioneer meteorologist. A very capable surveyor and hydrographer, he served as Governor of New Zealand from 1843-45, but he will be best remembered as the captain of HMS *Beagle* during Charles Darwin's famous second voyage of 1831–36.

Sir Philip Bowes Vere Broke (1776–1841) was born at Broke Hall near Nacton. His most notable achievement was his victory while in command of HMS *Shannon* over the capture of USS *Chesapeake* off Boston Massachusetts in June 1813, which created a sensation both sides of the Atlantic. A fictionalised account of Shannon's battle with *Chesapeake* is featured prominently in Patrick O'Brian's 'Master and Commander' novels, *The Fortune of War* and *The Surgeon's Mate*. In the novels, O'Brian makes Broke a cousin to his protagonist and hero, Captain Jack Aubrey.

BOYS AND GIRL OF THE OLD BRIGADE

Joseph Eley of Gedding served with the 38th Regiment and fought in twenty-nine engagements, including the Irish Rebellion, the Retreat of Sir John Moore to Corunna in 1809 during The Peninsular War, and was wounded at Waterloo. He died in May 1860 and is buried in Gedding churchyard.

James Hunt was one of the 7th Hussars present at the Battle of Waterloo and lived to the grand old age of 83 at Thornham Magna, where he died in May 1873.

Sergeant Alfred Ablett of the 3rd Battalion, Grenadier Guards, was one of the first recipients of the Victoria Cross, which he was awarded for his bravery at Sevastopol on 2 September 1855 during the Crimean War. He is buried in St Andrew's Churchyard, Weybread.

Private Henry Addison of the 43rd Regiment (Oxfordshire and Bucks Light Infantry), who was awarded the Victoria Cross for his gallantry during the Indian Mutiny in 1859, is buried in the churchyard of the church of St Peter & St Paul, Bardwell.

Sergeant John Hargreaves of the Royal Artillery served throughout the Crimean War and fought at Alma, Balaklava and Inkerman, where in this latter engagement he was the last man to leave his gun when his battery was stormed by the Russians. He was made a Knight of the French Légion d'honneur for his bravery and later became Drill Instructor to the Lowestoft Artillery Volunteers. Hargreaves died in May 1867 aged just 37, and was buried in St Margaret's churchyard in Lowestoft. A monument was erected to him by his comrades and friends from the town and neighbourhood.

Delia Jane Wilding was present with her husband William at the Battles of Alma, Balaclava, Inkerman and Sevastopol, where she attended to the wounded on the field of battle. Described by those who could recall her as 'a fine woman', five of her sons joined the army. Delia died at Old Newton in June 1894, aged 66, and was buried in Bacton churchyard.

Colonel James Morris Colquhon Colvin, of the Corps of Bengal Sappers and Miners, was awarded the Victoria Cross during the Mohmand Campaign in India 1897. He was cremated at Ipswich Crematorium.

General George Stracey Smyth (1767–1823) was *aide-de-camp* to Queen Victoria's father and died while acting as Lieutenant-Governor of New Brunswick in 1823. He had family connections with Suffolk and a memorial to his memory was erected in Chelsworth Church.

Private William Freestone of the 4th Light Dragoons, who was born at Needham Market, was a Suffolk Light Brigade 'charger' during the Battle of Balaclava on 25 October 1854. Uninjured during the charge, he later became a metropolitan policeman and was granted a special pension for injuries he received while on duty at Ascot Racecourse. Freestone spent the majority of his working life as the gatekeeper of the Wandsworth and Putney Gasworks.

Another Light Brigade 'charger' was Private Robert Briggs of the 11th Hussars who saved the life of Sergeant Seth Bond during the charge. Briggs was born and lived in Beccles most of his life, working as a coachman to Miss Lillistone. A familiar figure in the town, Briggs always wore his medals on Sundays and special occasions. He died in 1901.

Robert Stanmore, the last of fifty-seven Ipswich Crimean War veterans, died aged 98 on 27 August 1924.

Colonel Francis 'Frank' Rhodes CB, DSO (1851–1905), brother of the famous imperialist and politician Cecil Rhodes, was a distinguished soldier who served with distinction at the Relief of Khartoum. He was *The Times* war correspondent for Kitchener's Nile Expedition, was present at the Battle of El Teb and distinguished himself again at the Battle of Abu Klea.

He was captured by the Boers during the South African War and sentenced to death, a fate he only narrowly evaded with the payment of a hefty ransom, and still he returned to the colours and fought for The Relief of Mafeking. When peace came, he travelled hundreds of miles taking photographs of darkest Africa for a book describing the country from the Cape to the Zambesi. He died in Capetown in 1905 but was returned to Dalham for burial, where he had lived at the hall.

A WELCOME TO THE SUFFOLK VOLUNTEERS

The Riflemen are coming
To our good town to-day;
With heart and hand we'll greet them
With wreath and banner gay!

The cavalry may scout them.
The 'Regulars' may jeer
But Bury townsmen welcome in
The Suffolk Volunteer!

The Riflemen are coming!
Some hundreds strong they'll be;
Ye maids and matrons all, repair
The gallant sight to see!
And some I wis, will envy, (Though 'Regulars' may sneer)
The welcome Bury ladies give
The Suffolk Volunteer!

The Riflemen are coming
From Hadleigh and from Eye
From Sudbury and Mildenhall,
From places far and nigh –
Stowmarket, Brandon, Wickhambrook –
Brave hearts and true draw near;
Ring out, ring out, blithe Bury bells,
And greet each volunteer!

The Riflemen are coming!
Ay, let the joy-bells ring,
Although from vanquished foremen
No trophies now they bring;

Yet if in this, our island home
One hostile hand appear
'Ready, aye ready! Is the word
For ev'ry Volunteer.

The Riflemen are coming
To our good town to-day;
With heart and hand we'll greet them,
With wreath and banner gay;
The cavalry may taunt them,
The 'Regulars' may sneer,
But Britain's Queen with pride hath owned
Each loyal Volunteer!

(By Y.S.N., Bury, 14 June 1861)

THE BOER WAR MEMORIAL

The Boer War Memorial, which stands in the centre of Bury St Edmunds marketplace, bears the names of the 193 men of the county who fell in the South African War between 1899 and 1902. The memorial, by Arthur G. Walker, is surmounted by a figure with a rifle, and the sarcophagus upon which it stands was created by stonemason, Mr A.H. Hanchet. The memorial cost £750 and was unveiled on 11 November 1904 by General Lord Methuen.

HMS *GANGES*

The Royal Navy Training Establishment, Shotley, was opened as a shore-based training establishment for the training of boys entering the Royal Navy in 1905. At that time it was not customary to grant a shore establishment the title HMS, but the old HMS *Boscawen II* became HMS *Ganges* and held the 'Ships books'; thus, all the boys in training were technically aboard her and wore the cap tally of HMS *Ganges*.

To encourage and recognise high standards among the boys, the Shotley Medal was instituted. To gain the high distinction, a boy must be reported by all his officers as being 'V.G.' (Very Good) in all branches of his instructions and exceptionally distinguished in one of them, either in school, at work or on the field of athletics. The first boy to whom the medal was presented was Boy J. Keene in 1906.

The training mast of HMS *Ganges* stands 142ft high above the parade ground, and was erected in 1907. It comprises the foremast of HMS *Cordelia* and the topmast of HMS *Agincourt*. Set in a base on concrete 18ft deep, it has a further 60 tons of concrete clumps and pickets used to anchor the shrouds and stays, and has approx. 1 mile of rigging.

Mast manning, with its origins in sail, was the climbing of the rigging and lining the Yard arms by a total of eighty-one boys at a time. The manning was completed by the 'Button Boy' who would shin up to the very top and stand to attention on the 'truck' or 'button', 142ft above the parade ground, with only the lightning conductor to hold onto. He would be rewarded with the 'Captain's Shilling' (later a silver crown, a five shilling piece) on his return to the deck.

In 1967, BBC children's TV legend John Noakes took part in the Mast Manning at HMS *Ganges* but even he could not make it up the final section of the mast to be the 'Button Boy'.

At its zenith, HMS *Ganges* covered an area of nearly 102 acres.

Boys between the ages of 15 and 16 (16 years and 6 months in the case of grammar school boys) were recruited from across Great Britain and Ireland three times a term at intervals of five weeks.

The length of time a boy would spend in HMS *Ganges* in the 1950s depended on whether he was Seaman Branch, which was forty-one weeks, or Communications Branch, which took fifty-six weeks.

A TYPICAL DAY'S ROUTINE AT HMS *GANGES*, 1950

6.30 a.m.	Boys are called, sent to wash and have breakfast
7.40 – 8.40 a.m.	Clean the Establishment
8.40 a.m.	Divisions and Prayers
9.00 a.m.	Instruction begins
12.50 p.m.	Dinner
1.30 p.m.	Games, physical training, swimming, sailing and boat pulling
4.00 p.m.	Tea
4.40 – 6.40 p.m.	Instruction
6.50 p.m.	Supper
8.55 p.m.	All must be in bed and lights out.

There was no instruction on Wednesday and Saturday afternoons, or on Sundays.

Periodically, HM ships visited *Ganges* and the boys would be taken on board for a tour of inspection followed by a short sea trip, during which they could test their 'sea legs'.

The divisions of HMS *Ganges* were all named after notable naval personalities of the past. They were: Anson, Benbow, Blake, Drake, Frobisher, Hawke, Keppel and Rodney.

The daily rate of pay for a Boy 2nd Class on entry was 2*s* 6*d*, rising to 3*s* 6*d* on advancement to Boy 1st Class after approximately twenty-four weeks' service.

Admiral Sir Philip King Enright (1894–1960) and Rear Admiral Sir Benjamin Martin were both former HMS *Ganges* boys.

The White Ensign was lowered for the last time and HMS *Ganges* was finally paid off on 28 October 1976.

THE FUTURE KAISER DID VISIT FELIXSTOWE!

The German Empress Victoria and her son Crown Prince Wilhelm, then aged only 9, visited Felixstowe on 13 July 1881. They stayed for a few days enjoying the seaside, and even paid a quick visit to Queen Victoria, the boy's great-grandmother, in London. On 5 August, they eventually left on the Royal Yacht *Victoria and Albert*, which had been loaned to them.

FORT SUSSEX AT SOUTHWOLD

During the invasion scares of the First World War, the observation and patrol of the British Coast was entrusted to certain cycle and mounted corps of the Territorial Force. A Battalion of the Royal Sussex Regiment were given this duty for the strip of coastline around Southwold, and constructed a machine-gun post at Buss Creek, which they named Fort Sussex, exactly on the spot where a fort had been proposed to be built to repulse the Armada threat way back in 1588!

LOWESTOFT VICTORIA CROSS HERO

Royal Naval Reserve Skipper Thomas Crisp (1876–1917), recipient of the Victoria Cross and Distinguished Service Cross, was born and bred in Lowestoft. His VC citation stated:

> On the 15th August, 1917, the Smack 'Nelson' was engaged in fishing when she was attacked with gunfire from an enemy submarine. The gear was let go and the submarine's fire was returned. The submarine's fourth shot went through the port bow just below the water line and the seventh shell struck the skipper, partially disembowelling him, and passed through the deck and out through the side of the ship. In spite of the terrible nature of his wound Skipper Crisp retained consciousness, and his first thought was to send off a message that he was being attacked and giving his position. He continued to command his ship until the ammunition was almost exhausted and the smack was sinking. He refused to be moved into the small boat when the rest of the crew were obliged to abandon the vessel as she sank, his last request being that he might be thrown overboard.

The posthumous award of the Victoria Cross to Skipper Thomas Crisp, DSC, RNR was announced in the *London Gazette* on 2 November 1917.

THE WORST OF THE AIR RAIDS DURING THE GREAT WAR

On 12 August 1915, Woodbridge was bombed by a Zeppelin L.10 under the command of *Oberleutnant* Friedrich Wenke. The Zeppelin dropped four high-explosives and twenty incendiary bombs on the town, killing six and injuring twenty-four.

On 1 April 1916, Zeppelin L.16, under the command of *Oberleutnant* Werner Peterson, dropped eight explosives and a pair of incendiaries on Bury St Edmunds in the space of fifteen minutes, resulting in the death of seven people. The greatest tragedy was suffered by the Durball family. The father was away, serving with the Suffolk Regiment, when a bomb struck the family home on Mill Road. The bomb killed his wife and two of his children, the other three being nearly suffocated or injured. Hundreds of townspeople, civic dignitaries and soldiers lined the route for the main funeral for six of the casualties of the raid on 6 April. In this same raid, Zeppelin L.14 raided Sudbury, killing five people, while Zeppelin L.13 raided Stowmarket, where it was hit by anti-aircraft fire and sent on its way. This time, there was little damage caused to the town by the twelve high explosives it dropped.

On 4 July 1917, eighteen German Gotha Bombers attacked Felixstowe and Harwich at 7.30 a.m. Nine were killed and nineteen wounded at the Royal Naval Air Service base where a Curtiss H12 Flying Boat was also destroyed.

On 22 July 1917 the Gotha Bombers carried out a second attack, killing thirteen and injuring twenty-six. Most of the casualties in this raid were suffered by members of the Suffolk Regiment at a local army base. This was to be the worst night of casualties from air raids on Suffolk during the First World War.

RAIDER DOWN

The last Zeppelin to be shot down on British soil during the First World War landed on a field at Holly Tree Farm, Theberton, on 17 June 1917. Flying lower than was safe after an unsuccessful raid on Harwich, the L.48 Zeppelin, under the command of Kapitänleutnant Eichler, was brought down by machine-gun fire from pursuing British aircraft. Only three of the Zeppelin's crew survived the ensuing fireball and crash when the airship hit the ground. The wreckage was soon ringed by sentries to prevent souvenir hunters from taking their pick, and to hold back the crowds who came to see the wreckage. Large pieces of the Zeppelin still exist in museums in Suffolk and around the country; there are even sections of the frame on display in the porch of Theberton Church. Before their removal to Cannock Chase German Cemetery, the sixteen crew members that had perished were buried in Theberton cemetery, across the road from the churchyard. A plaque still marks the spot where they were buried and records the Royal Flying Corps chaplain's final words at the original committal: 'Who art thou that judgest another man's servant?'

THREE GREAT WAR FIGHTER ACES

Captain Henry Winslow, born in Southwold on 5 August 1895, the son of a local doctor, transferred from the infantry to 24 Squadron, Royal Flying Corps in 1916, and became famous for downing six enemy aircraft on 12 April 1918 while flying his 43 Squadron Sopwith Camel. By the end of the war, his confirmed tally was thirty-five: eleven balloons and twenty aircraft destroyed, and four aircraft sent out of control. He was decorated with the British Distinguished Service Order, Military Cross and Bar, as well as the French Légion d' honneur and Croix de Guerre. He was Suffolk's most decorated airman of the First World War.

Captain John Everard Gurdon, DFC, of 22 Squadron, Royal Flying Corps, was responsible for destroying thirteen enemy aircraft, one shared destruction and fourteen aircraft sent out of control, before he was commissioned into the Suffolk Regiment.

Lieutenant Percy Kyme Hobson MC, who scored seven victories flying an S.E. 5a with 84 Squadron, Royal Flying Corps, was born at Bungay on 20 November 1893.

STRANGERS

Three German prisoners of war escaped from a prison camp in Northamptonshire in April 1917. Somehow, the Germans, dressed in distinctly German civilian clothes and hardly disguising their heavy accents, managed to make their way by train to Halesworth. From there they attempted to walk to Southwold, where they intended to steal a boat and sail back to their homeland. On 30 April, PC Henry John Seaman was off duty and in plain clothes when he spotted these suspicious strangers, then walking on the road from Southwold to Wrentham. Stopping to question the men, he soon concluded they were at least 'aliens' and possibly spies. Arresting all three, they came quietly to Southwold Police Station, and the bold apprehension of the three runaways by a rural Suffolk 'bobby' became national news.

MASTERS OF MUNITIONS

The famous engineering firm Ransomes, Sims and Jefferies of Ipswich built no fewer than 650 aeroplane and airship hangars, 790 aeroplanes, 440,000 shell cases, 3 million parts for shells and fuses, 225 trench howitzers, 1,700 mines and 10,000 mortar bombs, as well as ploughs and agricultural equipment that helped to keep the country fed during the war.

THE FIRST HOME GUARD

During the First World War, the Volunteer Training Corps, in many ways a forerunner of the Home Guard of the Second World War, was raised across Britain to guard utilities and bridges from spies and saboteurs, and to keep a watchful eye over coastal areas in case of invasion. By the time of the Armistice, Suffolk had some 5,188 VTC volunteers.

LOSS OF A GENERATION

10,679 men of Suffolk fell in the First World War.

The names of 1,481 Ipswich service personnel who lost their lives during the First World War are inscribed on the town War Memorial on Christchurch Park.

At 147ft tall, Elveden War Memorial is one of the tallest in the country.

The village of Chelsworth lost just one man in the First World War, but still they did him proud by erecting a memorial to him in the parish church, inscribed: 'The people of Chelsworth erected this tablet in proud memory of Charles Peck, who gave his life for his country in the Great War, 25th September 1917, aged 19.'

Culpho is one of the fifty-two known 'Thankful Villages' of England and Wales – one of those rare places that lost no service personnel during the First World War. South Elmham, St Michael, may be doubly thankful, for all those who marched to war from that village returned in both the First and the Second World War.

SILKEN CANOPIES

The RAF's first parachute section was formed at Martlesham Heath by Flight Lieutenant John Potter, inventor of the Potter Parachute, assisted by Sergeant Hawking MM, Corporl East, and ten men known as the 'loonies'.

BAWDSEY RADAR

The world's first fully operational RADAR station opened at RAF Bawdsey on 24 September 1937. Bawdsey Manor Estate had been home to the top secret work of the 'Bawdsey Boffins' led by Robert Watson Watt and Arnold Wilkins since 1936, and they continued their development of radio direction finding there until the outbreak of war in September 1939, when the team was removed from this vulnerable coastal site to Dundee. RAF Bawdsey remained an important RADAR station and was later used as a Bloodhound Surface to Air Missile Site until its final closure on 31 March 1991.

THE RIDDLE OF SHINGLE STREET

On 7 September 1940, the 'Cromwell' code word (which warned of imminent German invasion) was given in error and scares of German parachutists and landings became rife across the country. From this date rumours began to circulate of large numbers of dead bodies, said to be German troops who had been burned severely, being washed ashore along the South-East Coast. One area where the stories of bodies on the beach in 1940 persist to this day is the Shingle Street area of Hollesley Bay. Had a German invasion force got caught in a flame barrage or had it been dealt with swiftly by the Royal Navy? Were the bodies actually those of British servicemen washed up after a training exercise went horribly wrong? Or was it all black propaganda to warn any potential invader and reassure the British public, in their 'darkest hour', of the anti-invasion defences of Great Britain? There are many questions that remain unanswered, but many ordinary people swore they saw numerous unexplained bodies washed up on the beaches in this area of Suffolk in September 1940.

STONE FRIGATES

The five naval bases of Lowestoft during the Second World War, otherwise known as the 'Stone Frigates', were HMS *Europa* (Royal Naval Patrol Service), HMS *Martello* (Mine-sweeping), HMS *Mantis* (Royal Navy Coastal Forces), HMS *Minos* (Harbour Defence) and HMS *Myloden* (Landing Craft Training for Royal Marines and Combined Operations).

ITALIANS OVER SUFFOLK

Felixstowe was one of the few places in Britain to have been bombed by Benito Mussolini's Italian Air Corps during the blitz of 1940.

Sergente Pilota Pietro Salvadori had his engine overheat in his biplane during a raid on Suffolk and had to make a forced landing on the shingle beach at Orford Ness on 11 November 1940. Salvadori was taken prisoner but remained immensely proud of his landing. His aircraft is now on display at the RAF Museum in London.

THE SHORT-LIVED LIFE OF HMS *FELIXSTOWE*

HMS *Felixstowe* was a Bangor class minesweeper launched in 15 January 1941. She was mined and sunk off Sardinia on 18 December 1943.

FEPOW HEROES

The men of the 4th and 5th Battalions of the Suffolk Regiment fought bravely along with their comrades in the 18th (Eastern) Division in the defence of the island of Singapore, but became prisoners of war after the surrender in February 1942. They went through hell at the hands of the Japanese; many lost their lives being worked like slaves building the infamous *Burma-Siam* 'Death Railway'. Many of those who survived suffered ill health and nightmares for the rest of their lives, but none of them ever forgot they were proud soldiers of the Suffolk Regiment.

MAPLE LEAF COMMANDER

Bury St Edmunds-born Lieutenant General Guy Granville Simonds (1903–1974) moved with his family to British Columbia in 1911. He entered as a cadet at the Royal Military College of Canada in 1921 and rose steadily through the ranks to become Commander of II Canadian Corps during the Second World War and the man who, as Acting Commander of the First Canadian Army, led Allied forces to victory at the Battle of the Scheldt in 1944. Simonds was appointed Chief of the General Staff, the most senior appointment of the Canadian Army, in 1951.

SECOND WORLD WAR
USAAF BASES IN SUFFOLK

1st Bombardment (later, 1 Air) Division 8th USAAF
356th Fighter Group, Martlesham Heath
364th Fighter Group, Honington

2nd Bombardment (later, 2nd Air) Division
Operated B-24D/H/J/L/M Liberators with 'Circle' tail codes until February 1944. Later designation was by various colour vertical tail fins with contrasting horizontal, vertical, or diagonal stripes designating a specific bomb group between late February 1944 and June 1945
446th Bombardment Group (Circle – H) Bungay
489th Bombardment Group (Circle – W) Halesworth

3rd Bombardment (later, 3rd Air) Division
Flew B17F/G Flying Fortresses with 'Square' tail codes February 1944 to July 1945
4th Combat Bombardment Wing Headquarters – Bury St Edmunds
94th Bombardment Group (Square – A) Bury St Edmunds
447th Bombardment Group (Square – K) Rattlesden
486th Bombardment Group (Square – 0/W) Sudbury
487th Bombardment Group (Square – P) Lavenham

13th Combat Bombardment Wing, Horham
390th Bombardment Group (Square – J) Framlingham
388th Bombardment Group (Square – H) Knettishall

93rd Combat Bombardment Wing, Mendlesham
34th Bombardment Group (Square – S) Mendlesham

385th Bombardment Group (Square – G) Great Ashfield
490th Bombardment Group (Square – T) Eye

66th Fighter Wing
353rd Fighter Group, Raydon
357th Fighter Group, Leiston

GLENN MILLER PLAYED HERE ...

Big band legend Major Glenn Miller, famous for such tunes as 'In the Mood', 'Moolight Serenade', 'American Patrol' and 'Pennsylvania 6-5000', played at numerous bases in hangars and in the open air for American Air Force personnel across East Anglia during 1944. Memories are that he played at far more bases than he really did, a situation confused because sometimes the Allied Expeditionary Forces Orchestra would play, but Glenn was not present. Or, as in one instance in the county, the notices and programmes were printed for Glenn and his orchestra to appear at Bury St Edmunds on 15 September 1944, but Glenn was unwell and the band was directed instead by drummer Sergeant Ray McKinley. What follows is a list of the confirmed Glenn Miller concerts in the county, for whom, where and when they were performed:

479th Fighter Group, Wattisham, 24 July 1944
489th Bomb Group, Halesworth, 6 August 1944
390th Bomb Group, Framlingham, 23 August 1944
388th Bomb Group, Knettishall, 25 August 1944
95th Bomb Group, Horham, 10 September 1944
385th Bomb Group, Great Ashfield, 1 October 1944

'HITCH' THE HERO

Royal Navy Coastal Forces hero Lieutenant-Commander Robert 'Hitch' Hitchens distinguished himself time and again during the Battle of the North Sea and was awarded the DSO and Bar, DSC, and two bars. He was mentioned in despatches three times and was also recommended for the Victoria Cross. Hitchens remains the most highly decorated officer of the Royal Naval Volunteer Reserve. He was killed in action on 13 April 1943, and is buried in Felixstowe cemetery.

THE RAF SERGEANT
WHO CAPTURED A BOMBER

In the early hours of 13 July 1944, a Luftwaffe Junkers 88-G1 bomber calmly landed at Woodbridge emergency aerodrome. After a brief struggle when the pilot and crew tried to destroy their papers, they were taken prisoner by the unarmed Sergeant Kenneth Clifton. When interrogated as to the reason for the course of his actions, the German pilot revealed he had been having problems with his navigation equipment, lost his bearings and believed he had landed in France!

3

SUFFOLK PEOPLE –
FAMOUS AND NOT
SO FAMOUS

Ronald 'Carl' Giles (1916–1995) was the cartoonist best known for his cartoons published in the *Daily Express*, many of which were featuring the extended Giles family, including 'Gran'. Giles worked in the town, lived nearby, was a keen supporter of Ipswich Town FC and died in Ipswich Hospital. A statue marking his long association with the town, featuring his character 'Gran', was erected on Queen Street in 1993, where she looks up at the newspaper office window where Giles used to work.

Simon Eyre was born in Brandon about 1395 and went to seek his fortune in London. He did well as a merchant and was a popular man, remembered in the history of the city of London for replacing the Leadenhall with a public granary, school and chapel in 1440. He was made Lord Mayor in 1445 and is often described as 'The Suffolk Dick Whittington'.

Photographer and influential artist Angus McBean (1904–1990), known for his photographic portraits of the likes of Elizabeth Taylor, Audrey Hepburn, Noel Coward and The Beatles, retired to Suffolk where he concentrated on the restoration of his moated house, Flemmings Hall, in Bedingfield near Eye, and owned an antique shop in Debenham.

Laurens van der Post, the prolific writer and novelist best known for his novel *The Seed and the Sower* (1963), reprinted as *Merry Christmas Mr Lawrence* and made into a film starring David Bowie and Tom Conti, lived for a number of years in Aldeburgh.

Humphry Repton (1752–1818), the man widely regarded as the last great English landscape designer, was born in Bury St Edmunds, the son of a collector of excise.

Sir Clement Freud (1924–2009), broadcaster, writer, politician, one of Britain's first celebrity chefs, and sadly missed stalwart of the Radio 4 comedy panel show *Just a Minute*, lived for many years in Walberswick and died there in 2009.

Neil Innes (1924–2019), singer, entertainer, musician and member of the Bonzo Dog Doo-Dah Band, lived in a farmhouse near Debenham.

Beryl Cook (1926–2008), the artist known for her saucy and humorous paintings, had the tenancy of a pub in Stoke by Nayland for a while.

John Le Mesurier (1912–1983), best remembered for his portrayal as Sergeant Arthur Wilson in the enduringly popular BBC comedy series *Dad's Army*, grew up in Bury St Edmunds.

Theatre and film director Sir Peter Hall was born at Bury St Edmunds in 1930. His notable film works include *A Midsummer Night's Dream* (1968), *The Homecoming* (1973), *Akenfield* (1974) and the television mini-series *The Camomile Lawn* (1992); he was also the presenter of the television arts series *Aquarius* (1975–76).

Elton Hayes, actor, singer and guitarist best known for his recordings of an arrangement of Edward Lear's *The Owl and The Pussycat*, who also had his own television shows *Elton Hayes – He Sings to a Small Guitar*, *Close Your Eyes* and *Tinker's Tales*, spent his last years in Bury St Edmunds, where he died in 2001.

Royal Academy-exhibited portrait painter Rose Mead was born the daughter of a Bury St Edmunds plumber and glazier in 1867. During the 1890s she painted a self-portrait in the act of cooking. A company that made similar cookers offered her £500, about £40,000 in modern money, to add their name to the appliance but she refused because she was unwilling to 'prostitute' her art. Rose returned to Bury in later life and was found dead at the bottom of her studio stairs on Crown Street in March 1946.

Trevor Nunn, has directed musicals on Broadway and in the West End, opera at Glyndebourne and has been artistic director for both the Royal Shakespeare Company and Royal National Theatre was born at Ipswich in 1949 and was educated at Northgate Grammar School.

Benjamin Britten (1913–1976), the composer best known for *Peter Grimes* and *The Young Person's Guide to the Orchestra* and founder of the Aldeburgh Festival of Music, was born on Kirkley Cliff Road, Lowestoft, and was the son of a local dentist. Britten spent his last years in Horham, where he wrote *Phaedra*, *Death in Venice*, the *Third String Quartet* and the orchestral suite *A Time There Was*. He died on 4 December 1976 and was buried in Aldeburgh cemetery on 7 December 1976.

Joseph Priestley (1733–1804), dissenting clergyman, theologian, natural philosopher, author of 150 works, and one of the men credited with the discovery of oxygen – which he described as 'dephlogisticated air' – had his first parish at Needham Market in 1755.

Thomas Clarkson, one of the founders of The Society for Effecting the Abolition of the Slave Trade and one of those who helped achieve the passing of the Slave Trade Act in 1807, spent his later years at Playford Hall and died there aged 86 on 26 September 1846. He is buried in St Mary's Church, Playford, and an obelisk to his memory was erected in the churchyard in 1857.

Sybil Andrew (1898–1992), an artist known for her modernist linocuts, was born in Bury St Edmunds.

John Bale (1495–1563) was a Covehithe man who became the last Prior of the Ipswich Carmelite House and went on to be made Bishop of Ossory under Edward VI. He retired as the Prebendary of Canterbury, and was a man with such a reputation for an unhappy disposition and the bitterness of his tongue in argument that he acquired the nickname of 'Bilious Bale'.

River Monsters presenter, biologist and extreme angler Jeremy Wade was born in Suffolk.

Novelist Maria Louise Ramé (she preferred to be known as Marie Louise de la Ramée) (1839–1908), who wrote under the pseudonym of Ouida, was born in Bury St Edmunds. She produced over forty novels, children's books and collections of short stories and essays, two of which have been turned into films – *Under Two Flags* (1867) with film versions produced in 1912, 1916, a 1922 version directed by Tod Browning and another in 1936 starring Ronald Colman and Claudette Colbert. The other was *A Dog in Flanders* (1872), which had English film versions made in 1935, 1959 and in 1999, starring Jon Voight.

The 1980s pop star Nik Kershaw, known for 'The Riddle' and 'Wouldn't it be Good', which reached No. 3 and No. 4 respectively in the UK singles chart in 1984, grew up in Ipswich.

Physicist Lawrence Bragg was best known for his work in x-ray crystallography and for proposing what is now known as Bragg's law of diffraction in 1912. With his father, William, they shared the Nobel Prize for Physics in 1915 when he was still in his twenties. Lawrence Bragg remains the youngest Nobel laureate in history. He died at Ipswich in 1971.

Richard Hakluyt, author of *Divers Voyages Touching the Discoverie of America* (1582) and *The Principal Navigations, Voyages, Traffiques and Discoveries of the English Nation* (1589–1600), was rector of Wetheringsett-cum-Brockford in the 1590s.

Artist and sculptor Ellen Mary Rope was born at Grove Farm, Blaxhall. Active in the decorative arts, she designed for the Della Robbia Pottery, Birkenhead, from 1886 until its closure in 1906. Her work was very much in the Arts and Crafts movement tradition and was seen at each Arts and Crafts Exhibition Society exhibition from 1889, and can be found in Winchester and Salisbury Cathedrals, as well as in the church of her home village of Blaxhall. Retiring to her family farm in the 1920s, she died in 1934 aged 79 and was buried in Blaxhall churchyard.

Field Marshal Horatio Herbert, Earl Kitchener (1850–1916), the national hero and Secretary of State for War appointed at the start of the First World War, whose imposing moustached face and pointing finger was used to great effect in the 'Your Country Needs You' recruitment posters, had close family connections with Suffolk; his mother, Frances Anne, was a Chevallier of Aspall, and she is buried in the parish church. Indeed, when Kitchener was elevated to the peerage he styled himself Earl Kitchener of Khartom and Aspall.

Admiral Horatio Nelson's mother was born Catherine Suckling in the rectory at Barsham on 9 May 1725.

Captain Francis Light (1740–1794), the founder of Penang, Malaya, was born and baptised at Dallinghoo and was brought up at Woodbridge Grammar School. His son, William, went on to found Adelaide in Australia.

Justin Hawkins, the falsetto-voiced flamboyant frontman of the rock band The Darkness, grew up in Lowestoft and attended Kirkley High School.

Ronald Blythe, the editor and author best known for his 1969 classic *Akenfield: Portrait of an English Village*, was born in Acton in 1922.

Arthur Young (1741–1820), the prominent writer on agriculture, economics and social statistics, was born at Bradfield Combust and was schooled at Lavenham. His observations based on his travels through the agricultural areas of England and Wales were published in the books *A Six Weeks' Tour through the Southern Counties of England and Wales*, *A Six Months' Tour through the North of England* and the *Farmer's Tour through the East of England*, published between 1768 and 1770. He went on to travel in Ireland and France and published more titles such as *Farmer's Calendar*, which went through numerous editions. He began to edit *Annals of Agriculture* in 1784, which were continued through forty-five volumes. He lies buried in Bradfield Combust.

Reginald Livesey, the respected explorer and cartographer who explored the interior of Queensland, Australia, and studied the bird life of Pacific Islands, died at Brundish Manor, Suffolk, aged 78, in 1932.

Brian Eno – full name Brian Peter George St John le Baptiste de la Salle Eno – musician, composer, record producer and singer, and one of the foremost innovators in ambient music, was born at the Phyllis Memorial Hospital, Woodbridge, in 1948 and still owns a house in the town.

Sir Robert Hitcham (1572–1636), although born in humble circumstances at Levington, showed promise as a student at the Free School at Ipswich and passed as a pensioner to Pembroke Hall, Cambridge. He took up Law and held a number of prestigious offices, including Attorney-General to Anne of Denmark, received a knighthood and became Senior Sergeant-at-Law to James I. Hitcham's Cloister in Pembroke College (built in 1666) is named in his honour. Sir Robert is buried in Framlingham Church.

Mary Rose Tudor, the youngest sister of Henry VIII to live past childhood, and who became the princess who married Louis XII of France, married her one true love, Charles Brandon, Duke of Suffolk after she became a widow. When she died in 1533 her body was interred in the Bury St Edmunds Abbey and moved for safekeeping to St Mary's Church after the abbey was dissolved in 1540.

Miss Nina Layard was the first woman to read a paper before the Royal Archaeological Institute. Their meeting was held, on this occasion, at Ipswich Town Hall on 26 July 1899, and Miss Layard spoke on her research into the unknown sites of the religious houses in the town.

Charles Austin (1799–1874), born the second son of Jonathan Austin of Creeting Mill, became regarded, along with his friend, the historian Thomas Macaulay, as one of the best talkers of his generation. Austin did not achieve the fame of Macaulay but he did make a fortune at the Bar. He died at Brandeston Hall, near Wickham Market, and is buried in the local cemetery.

Mary Beale (1632–1699), the first female English professional painter and one who has been described as one of the best female painters of the seventeenth century, was born at Barrow, near Bury St Edmunds.

Marharajah Duleep Singh (1838–1893) made his home at Elveden Hall in 1863. He restored the 17,000-acre estate, its cottages, the village church, the school and remodelled the old hall into a quasi-oriental palace, where he lived the life of a British aristocrat and gained the reputation of being the fourth best shot in England.

George Page, 'The Suffolk Giant', died in April 1870 aged 26. Born and buried at Newbourne, George had grown to stand over 7ft tall. Along with his brother, Meadows, who was also over 7ft tall, they joined George Whiting's travelling fair in May 1869 and travelled the country, being put on show as living curiosities.

Stage and screen actress Jane Lapotaire, who has appeared in such films as *Antony and Cleopatra* (1972), *Shooting Fish* (1997) and *There's Only One Jimmy Grimble* (2000), was born in Ipswich in 1944.

Academy award-winning stage and screen actor Ralph Fiennes, best known for his big screen performances in *Schindler's List* (1993) *The Constant Gardener* (2005) and as Lord Voldemort in the *Harry Potter* films, was born in Ipswich in 1962 (he did not live there though, he and his parents lived near Southwold).

'Travel Man', comedian and comic actor Richard Ayoade, known for his performances as Dean Learner in *Garth Marenghi's Darkplace*, *Man to Man with Dean Learner* and as Maurice Moss in *The IT Crowd*, was raised in Ipswich.

Henry Bunbury (1750–1811) was an amateur artist and caricaturist regarded as 'The West Suffolk Hogarth'. Born at Mildenhall, he married and settled at Barton Hall. Many of his character studies were inspired by the characters he saw in nearby Bury St Edmunds. Bunbury exhibited at the Royal Academy from 1780 to 1808.

Maggi Hambling, contemporary figurative painter, print maker and sculptor, best known locally for her creation of *The Scallop* on Aldeburgh beach, was born in Sudbury in 1945.

Jack Rose (1926–2000) really was 'Mr Lowestoft' – his knowledge and memories made him an outstanding historian of the town and quite a character in his own right. He would welcome anyone with a genuine interest in the history of the town into his Crown Street home, and shared his knowledge and pictures with wider audiences through his slide shows, helping raise money for many good causes. When the Old Lowestoft Society was disbanded, a new society was created in 1990, with Jack as president. I am sure he would be pleased to know The Jack Rose Old Lowestoft Society is still going and his books about the town are still enjoyed today.

John Peel (1939–2004), real name John Robert Parker Ravenscroft, one of the most influential and best-loved radio presenters of the twentieth century, lived in Great Finborough, Suffolk, for thirty-three years and is buried at St Andrew's Church in the village.

Thomas Gainsborough (1727–1788), the outstanding portrait and landscape painter, known for such masterpieces as *The Blue Boy*, *The Morning Walk* and *Mr and Mrs Robert Andrews*, was born the son of a weaver and maker of woollen goods in Sudbury, and lived with his wife and family in Ipswich between 1752 and 1759.

John Constable (1776–1837), the landscape painter, was born in East Bergholt. He became renowned for such works as *The Hay Wain* and other paintings that so evocatively captured Dedham Vale and have caused this beautiful area to become known as 'Constable Country'.

Sir Alfred Munnings (1878–1959), one of England's finest painters of horses in rural, military or sporting settings, was born at Mendham. Some of Munning's earliest commissions came from Shaw Tomkins, who commissioned him to design posters and boxes for chocolates. Munnings went on to become president of the Royal Academy of Art in 1944. His work is appreciated all over the world and continues to increase in value, and as of 2007, the highest price paid for a Munnings painting was $7,848,000, for *The Red Prince Mare*.

Twiggy, one of the world's most iconic and enduring models, lives in Southwold with her actor-husband, Leigh Lawson.

Versatile actor Brian Capron, who has appeared in a host of long-running and successful TV shows and series, including *Z-Cars*, *Grange Hill*, and *Blake's 7*, *Tales of the Unexpected*, *Bergerac* and *Coronation Street*, was born in Eye.

Ed Sheeran, the singer-songwriter best known for his hits 'Give Me Love', 'The A Team' and 'Lego House', spent much of his young life in Framlingham.

Delia Smith, one of Britain's best-loved and most practical celebrity cooks, lives near Stowmarket.

Irish-born actor Tony Scannell (1945–2020), best known for his long-running portrayal of DS Ted Roach in the ITV police drama series *The Bill*, lived for many years with his wife and family in Suffolk.

TV soap icon June Brown, best known for her role as Dot Cotton in *Eastenders*, was born at Needham Market in 1927.

Dani Filth (born Daniel Lloyd Davey), singer and founding member of the heavy metal band Cradle of Filth, lives in the county and married his wife, Toni, in Ipswich in 2005.

Sir Proby Thomas Cautly (1802–1871), the palaeontologist and engineer best known for conceiving and overseeing the construction of the 350-mile long Ganges canal in India, was born in Suffolk.

Bob Hoskins, the actor best known for his cockney hard man roles in such films as *The Long Good Friday*, *Mona Lisa*, and TV dramas like *Pennies from Heaven*, was born at Bury St Edmunds in 1942.

Hip hop, R&B and grime DJ and TV presenter Tim Westwood, best known as the presenter of *Pimp My Ride UK*, and whose discography includes 'Street Beats', 'Westwood Volume 1', 'Westwood: The Jump Off', and 'Westwood 7: The Big Dawg', was born at Lowestoft in 1957, the son of Bill Westwood, former Anglican Bishop of Peterborough.

James 'Jimmy' Hoseason (1927–2009), one of East Anglia's most successful and well-known holiday entrepreneurs, was born at South Cove, near Southwold, and spent his early years in Lowestoft where his father, Wally, was the harbourmaster. In fact, it was Wally who started the business when he began hiring out boats on Oulton Broad on behalf of their owners as holiday homes late in the Second World War. When Wally died in 1950, Jimmy took over the company and built it up to sell £100 million worth of holidays a year and employed 10,000 people on 100 boatyards and holiday parks. When Hoseason retired in 1999 he sold the company for £22 million in a management buyout.

Musical theatre actress and singer Kerry Ellis was born in the village of Haughley, near Stowmarket, in 1979.

Elizabeth Garrett Anderson (1836–1917), the first Englishwoman to qualify as a physician and surgeon in Britain, is also co-founder of the first hospital to be staffed by women. She was appointed Mayor of Aldeburgh in 1908, and she was the first woman in the country to hold such a position. Her sister, Dame Millicent Garrett Fawcett (1847–1929), was a leading women's suffrage campaigner, author, academic and political leader.

THE SON OF AN IPSWICH BUTCHER

Thomas Wolsey was born the son of an affluent Ipswich butcher and owner of property in around 1473. Rising up through the ranks of the church he was chaplain to, he was then made cardinal by King Henry VIII. A master administrator, Wolsey exercised a marked influence on affairs of State, and King Henry VIII followed his counsel and entrusted more power to his hands, appointing him to the ultimate state accolade of Lord Chancellor in 1515, a position Wolsey held until a year before his death. Wolsey was not liked by the public; he had aroused public hostility with his financial exactions and provoked the enmity of all by the extravagant pomp he surrounded himself with on public occasions. His origins were used as a term of derision behind his back by many at court, referring

to him as 'son of a butcher'. By 1529, Wolsey was felt by Henry to be 'failing his king'. Wolsey really fell from favour after he failed to get the annulment of the King's marriage to Catherine of Aragon. Wolsey died while being escorted by the King's Commissioners to the Tower of London, where he was to answer to charges of High Treason. His passing was unlamented by all, except those in his closest retinue.

THE ICONOCLAST

William Dowsing was responsible for the destruction of more church decorations, fixtures and fittings than any other man. Born in Laxfield in 1596, he was appointed 'Visitor of the Churches of Suffolk' by the Earl of Manchester in 1644. His mission: 'To destroy and abolish all remains of popish superstition in them.' The journal of William Dowsing records over 150 visits to town and country churches, where he did far more than sign the visitors' book. Included among the entries are Haverhill, where among the total of 300 images and symbols on glass, wood, brass and stone that were destroyed he particularly noted the destruction of a picture of '… seven Fryars hugging a nun'. A typical days work for Dowsing is recorded thus:

At Clare ... we brake down 1000 pictures superstitious; I brake down 200; 3 of God the Father, and 3 of Christ, and the Holy Lamb, and 3 of the Holy Ghost like a Dove with wings; and the 12 Apostles were carved in wood, on the top of the Roof, which we gave order to take down; and 20 Cherubims to be taken down; and the Sun and Moon in the East Window, by the King's Arms, to be taken down.

ROBINSON CRUSOE

Thomas Colson, an eccentric character of Ipswich, more generally known as Robinson Crusoe, was a former stocking weaver who became a fisherman on the Orwell. His boat was a mass of patches, and to eke his meagre living he fished in all weathers. 'Subject to violent chronic complaints, and his mind somewhat distempered, his figure tall and thin, with meagre countenance and piercing blue eyes', he was aptly described:

> With squalid garments round him flung,
> And o'er his bending shoulders hung
> A string of perforated stones
> With knots of elm and horses bones.
>
> He dreams that wizards, leagued with hell
> Have o'er him cast their deadly spell,
> Though pinching pains his limbs endure,
> He holds his life by charms secure,
> And while he feels the torturing ban,
> No wave can drown the spell-bound man.

Tragically, his boat was driven onto 'The Ooze' by a storm on 3 October 1811. Convinced of the efficacy of the charms he surrounded himself with, Colson obstinately refused to leave his vessel, and so when the ebb tide came, he and his little boat were swept into deep water and he sank to rise no more.

GUNPOWDER PLOTTER

One of the 1605 Gunpowder Plot conspirators, Ambrose Rookwood (*c.* 1578–1606), was probably born and spent much of his young life in the village of Stanninghall, where his family had lived for generations.

Arrested, tried and found guilty of his involvement in the plot, Rookwood was hanged, drawn and quartered in the Old Palace Yard, Westminster, along with Thomas Wintour, Robert Keyes and Guy Fawkes on 31 January 1606.

WHO WAS MARGARET CATCHPOLE?

One of the most famous women in the history of Suffolk is Margaret Catchpole, made famous by the Revd Richard Cobbold's book which bore her name. She made her escape from Ipswich Gaol in March 1800. The original notice which offered £5 (rather than Cobbold's inflated £20) for her capture stated that she made her escape at a place where the spikes of the *chevaux de frise* was broken, reaching it by means of a garden frame, linen crotch and line. Using these simple aids she scaled the 22ft wall, tied the linen line to the frame of the *chevaux de frise*, slid under the 10in gap left by the broken spike and let herself down with the line on the other side. The notice concludes: 'This extraordinary escape is only worthy of such an extraordinary character as Margaret Catchpole, who stole a horse, and afterwards rode off with it to London, a distance of 70 miles in 10 hours.' For the theft of the horse, she was tried and condemned to death at Bury Assizes in 1797, a sentence later commuted to seven years' transportation. She was transported to Australia, where she died unmarried (but not without having received numerous offers) on 13 May 1819, aged 57. She may have not been the beauty created by Cobbold, and Will Laud, the smuggler lover that she rode to London for, may not have existed, but the facts of her remarkable ride, escape and life after transportation are well-attested truths. *The History of Margaret Catchpole, A Suffolk Girl* has been reprinted many times and still remains a thumping good read.

PLEASANT LADY PLEASANCE

Lady Pleasance Smith, wife of James Smith, the founder of the Linnean Society, was born in Lowestoft in 1773. A woman known for her great beauty in her youth, kindness, stately presence and longevity, she lived on for almost forty-nine years after the death of her husband. She edited a posthumous selection of Smith's letters, published in 1832, and returned to the town of her birth in 1849, making her home in a house on the High Street. Lady Smith died in her 105th year in 1877. A window was erected to her memory in St Margaret's Church, Lowestoft.

A FRIEND INDEED

The Revd John Stevens Henslow (1796–1861), rector of Hitcham for twenty years, strove to help the local people turn the living and working conditions of their agricultural parish into a happy and productive one. He began by establishing a parish school and The Hitcham Labourers' and Mechanics' Horticultural Society for the education of adults. He also set up a number of charities in the village to help those in dire need. He worked with the farmers to improve the quality of their soil and encouraged team work, good neighbourliness and public interaction by inaugurating all manner of competitive and social events, from ploughing matches and the creation of a cricket club to 'parish treats' (organised days out), firework displays in the rectory lawn and magic lantern shows. He is affectionately remembered there as 'The Farm Labourer's Friend', but he will be best known to the rest of the world as the friend and mentor to his pupil – Charles Darwin.

4

THAT'S ENTERTAINMENT

WHAT WAS FILMED WHERE?

The popular 1980s series charting the adventures of lovable rogue and antiques dealer Lovejoy, played by Ian McShane, was filmed extensively in Suffolk at locations such as Bildeston, Bury St Edmunds (including the Angel Hotel), Hadleigh, Kersey, Long Melford and Sudbury. The home of Lady Jane Felsham, Lovejoy's romantic interest, known in the series as Felsham Hall, was not in the Suffolk village but was, in fact, Belchamp Hall at Belchamp Walter in Essex. The final episode of the series aired in 1994 was entitled 'Last Tango in Lavenham', and included a number of scenes in the village.

In the film *Barry Lindon* (1975), which starred Ryan O'Neil, Hardy Kruger and Patrick Magee, the inn where Barry had to endure the amputation of his leg after a duel was the Guildhall in Lavenham.

Lavenham was used as Godric's Hollow in *Harry Potter and the Deathly Hallows*.

In *Witchfinder General* (1968), starring Vincent Price, a number of locations were used in Suffolk including Knettishall Heath, Dunwich, Brandeston and notably Kentwell Hall in Long Melford, where the bridge over the moat was used for the ducking scene, and Lavenham marketplace, where the infamous witch-burning scene was shot. The climax of the film was also shot in the county, at Orford Castle.

Classic BBC comedy *Dad's Army* was filmed at a number of locations in Suffolk, including Honington, Bardwell, Beccles, Brandon, Drinkstone Mill and Lowestoft.

Kentwell Hall was used for Toad Hall, the home of Mr Toad, in *The Wind in the Willows* (1996).

The Market Square at Lavenham is the setting for John Lennon and Yoko Ono's film *Apotheosis* (1970).

The exotic interior of Elveden Hall became the interior of villain Manfred Powell's mansion in *Lara Croft: Tomb Raider* (2001), starring Angelina Jolie. It was the Stormhold where the old king, played by Peter O'Toole, lay on his deathbed in *Stardust* (2007), and in the James Bond film, *The Living Daylights* (1987), it was supposedly Tangiers, Morocco, for a banquet scene. It was also used for the orgy scene in Stanley Kurbrick's *Eyes Wide Shut* (1999).

In the James Bond film *Tomorrow Never Dies* (1997), the US airbase at 'Okinawa, in the South China Sea' is RAF Lakenheath.

The Chief (1990–1995), one of the last locally made Anglia TV drama series, used East Anglian, or rather the fictional Eastland Police district, as the setting for its stories, one of which included the take-over of Bawdsey Manor (with police marksmen on the roof) for a fictional 'Europol' international police conference. Bawdsey Manor was also used for exterior and interiors for the BBC drama series *Insiders*.

The Scouting Book for Boys (2009), starring Thomas Turgoose and Holliday Grainger, was filmed around the Broadland Sands Holiday Park in Corton, Suffolk.

The BBC soap opera *The Newcomers* (1965–1969), set in the fictional country town of Angleton, used Haverhill to shoot its external scenes.

The CBeebies pre-school comedy drama series *Grandpa in My Pocket*, set in the fictional location of Sunnysands, uses exteriors at Aldeburgh and Southwold, including the pier and the lighthouse.

The war movie *Yangtse Incident: The Story of HMS Amethyst* (1956), starring Richard Todd and William Hartnell, was filmed just off Shotley Gate.

The beach scenes for *Iris* (2001), the story of novelist Iris Murdoch, starring Dame Judi Dench, were filmed at Southwold.

The Fourth Protocol (1987), starring Michael Caine and Pierce Brosnan, includes a car chase filmed around Ipswich and a helicopter flying under the Orwell Bridge.

In *Beau Brummell* (1954), starring Stewart Granger, the horse racing meet was filmed at Newmarket Racecourse.

An episode of *Randell and Hopkirk (Deceased)* (1967), named 'The Trouble with Women', sees Jeff Randell (Mike Pratt) and his ghostly partner Marty Hopkirk (Kenneth Cope) at Newmarket Racecourse.

Roald Dahl's *Tales of the Unexpected* (1979), the classic episode entitled 'Neck', starring Joan Collins, Michael Aldridge, Peter Bowles and John Gielgud, was filmed at Somerleyton Hall.

The ITV drama *A Mother's Son* (2012), starring Hermione Norris, Martin Clunes and Paul McGann, was filmed in and around Southwold and Walberswick.

Framlingham Castle featured in an episode entitled 'The Path of True Love' in *The Adventures of Robin Hood* (1957), starring Richard Greene.

The Champions (1968) episode entitled 'The Final Countdown' includes a scene with Sharron Macready (Alexandra Bastedo) and Richard Barrett (William Gaunt) at Kersey.

Ha'penny Breeze (1950), starring Don Sharpe, was filmed in and around Pin Mill.

The public information film *Spring Offensive* (1940) about the role of War Agricultural Committees was filmed at Moat Farm, Clopton.

The Children's Film Foundation film *The Secret of the Forest* (1955) was shot in and around Rendlesham.

The filming for the Peter Hall film *Akenfield* (1974), based on Ronald Blythe's book *Akenfield: Portrait of an English Village* (1969), used the village of Charsfield as one of its main locations.

The Peter Greenaway film *Drowning by Numbers* (1988), starring Joan Plowright, Juliet Stephenson and Joely Richardson, used locations at Southwold, Thorpeness and the River Blyth.

Michael Palin's drama *East of Ipswich* (1987) was filmed at Southwold.

The British Council film *Lowland Village* (1942) was filmed in Kersey and Lavenham.

This Was England (1937) is a wonderful film and social documentary charting the history of farming and old farming methods in Suffolk. It was made by pioneering educational film maker Mary Field.

Part of the 'Jason King' episode from *A Thin Band of Air* (1971), starring Peter Wyngarde, was filmed at Manning's Amusement Park in Felixstowe.

The docudrama film *Village in the Wheatfields* (1949) charted the farming year in the villages of Rickinghall Inferior and Rickinghall Superior.

In the first series finale of BBC spy drama *Spooks* (2002), the exterior of Sizewell nuclear power station was used for the fictional Sefton B power station.

BBC murder mystery series *Jonathan Creek*, starring Alan Davies, has scenes filmed at Wangford and Wrentham.

CINEMA STARS

Suffolk's oldest surviving purpose-built cinema is Leiston Picture House (now known as Leiston Film Theatre), opened in October 1914.

The Electric Picture Palace at Southwold first opened on York Road in 1912. After the closure of the old cinema the new Electric Picture palace, complete with authentic cinema seats, box office, circle and organ, was opened by Michael Palin in May 2002.

The Aldeburgh Cinema has been screening films since 1919, when the auditorium was built on the back of a High Street shop. For forty of those years, Mr Neville Parry has been projectionist, and at 80 is believed to be the oldest projectionist in the country.

SOME LOST CINEMAS OF SUFFOLK

The Cinema, Saltgate, Beccles
The Regal, Ballygate, Beccles
The Brandon Cinema, The Avenue, Brandon
The Mayfair, Bungay
The Playhouse, The Buttermarket, Bury St Edmunds
The Empire, Bell Arcade, Bury St Edmunds
The Gem, St Johns Street, Bury St Edmunds
Victoria Hall, Victoria Parade, Felixstowe
The Regal, Framlingham
The Palace, 112 High Street, Hadleigh
Electric Empire, High Street, Haverhill
Central Cinema, Princes Street, Ipswich
Empire, Fore Street, Ipswich
Picture House, Tavern Street, Ipswich
Ideal, Lavenham
Kinnodrome, Kessingland
Palace Cinema, Royal Terrace, Lowestoft
Cosy Corner, High Street, Lowestoft
Coronet, London Road North, Lowestoft
Electric Cinema, Mildenhall
Kingsway Cinema, High Street, Newmarket
County Cinema, Sudbury

FISHER'S THEATRES

In the late eighteenth and early nineteenth centuries, Suffolk and Norfolk theatrical entertainment was dominated by the Fisher family and their Norfolk and Suffolk Company of Comedians. They were welcomed by upstanding members of society in both counties, and as the troupe grew in size and stature, David Fisher, the head of the Company, decided that it was profitable enough that instead of setting up his plays in inadequate playhouses, he could start to buy, enlarge and improve them and even build them anew to his own designs. Completing his first two theatres in 1812, Fisher then financed more over the next sixteen years by raising capital with share offerings to local patrons. Fisher created his own 'circuit' of thirteen theatres across both counties, specifically, the theatres in the following towns:

Halesworth
Lowestoft (2 theatres)

Wells-Next-the-Sea
Woodbridge

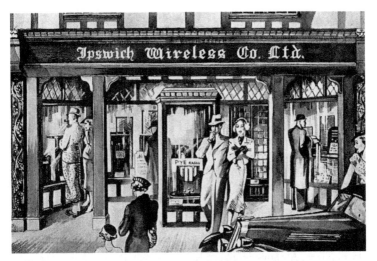

Eye	Swaffham
East Dereham Sudbury	Newmarket
Thetford	Bungay
Beccles	North Walsham

RADIO IN SUFFOLK

Radio Orwell, launched in Ipswich on 28 October 1975, was the first independent local radio station to open in East Anglia.

BBC Radio Suffolk began broadcasting on 12 April 1990.

BBC Radio Suffolk broadcaster Rob Dunger formerly worked as a florist and is fluent in French, Spanish and Dutch.

James Hazell has advanced skills in computer programming and spent three years at BT Research in Martlesham Heath.

BBC Radio Suffolk's Mark Murphy was awarded the Sony Gold award for 'New Broadcaster of the Year' in 2003.

Radio Suffolk was named 'Station of the Year' at the Sony Radio Awards in 2004.

Amber Radio first broadcast on 24 September 1995.

Saxon Radio first came to air in Bury St Edmunds on 6 November 1982.

103.4 The Beach, based in Lowestoft studios, broadcast for the first time on 29 September 1996.

ANGLIA TELEVISION TRIVIA TREASURES

Anglia Television first went on air on 27 October 1959.

Anglia's first newsreaders were 'Sandy' Newman Sanders, Drew Russell and Colin Bower.

Anglia's flagship nature documentary series *Survival* was first broadcast in 1961 and ran to over 900 episodes. The distinguished narrators for the programme over the years included Orson Welles, Henry Fonda, David Niven, Anthony Hopkins, Robert Powell, Dennis Waterman, and HRH Prince Phillip.

Fondly remembered pre-school children's show *Romper Room* ran between 1964 and 1977. The presenters were Miss Rosalyn (Rosalyn Thompson, 1964–1976) and Biddy Massen. Despite reaching the shortlist of six applicants to be the original presenter, Esther Rantzen didn't get the job.

Anglia produced the first version of *Mr and Mrs* in 1969, with Norman Vaughan as compère.

Sale of The Century, presented by Nicholas Parsons, ran between 1971 and 1983. The iconic theme tune 'Joyful Pete' (named so in a gesture to the Director Peter Joy) was composed by Peter Fenn, director of music at Anglia, who played live on his organ at every recording.

Another award-winning Anglia quiz show was *Gambit*, based on the card game pontoon and was hosted by Fred Dinenage (1975–1982) and Tom O'Connor (1983–1985) featuring Miss Anglia finalist Michelle Lambourne as hostess on almost every episode.

The popular *Bygones* series was presented by affectionately remembered Anglia personality Dick Joice from 1967 until his retirement in 1987.

The famous drawing room introduction scene for each of the Roald Dahl *Tales of the Unexpected* was actually filmed in a specially designed set in a studio at Anglia House.

'BC', the playful leopard cub puppet who 'helped' the *Birthday Club* presenter sort the cards, first appeared in 1980.

Anglia weathermen included Jim Bacon, David Brooks, Peter Walker, Eric Dudley, Colin Corkerton, Andy Cutcher and Michael Hunt.

LITERARY SUFFOLK

Prolific author R. Thurston Hopkins (1884–1958), whose father had been an official with the Commisioner of Prisons, spent much of his young life at Gyves House in the walls of the old prison at Bury St Edmunds. Although he did write on topography, biographical studies

and other subjects, he will be best remembered for his books on ghosts with such titles as *Adventures with Phantoms* (1946), *Ghosts Over England* (1953) and *Cavalcade of Ghosts* (1956).

George Orwell, born Eric Arthur Blair (1903–1959), lived with his family in Southwold when they moved after his father's retirement, and had long and short stays in the town for many years. His book *A Clergyman's Daughter*, based on his life as a teacher, includes some of his experiences there.

Richardson Pack, 'The Soldier Poet', was born at Stoke Ash on 29 November 1682.

George Crabbe (1754–1832), surgeon, coleopterist and clergyman – though best remembered as a poet – was born in Aldeburgh, Suffolk and first developed his love of poetry in the town.

Robert Bloomfield (1766-1823), the poet best known for 'The Farmer's Boy', was born into a humble family at Honington.

Thomas Nashe, pamphleteer and one of the fathers of modern journalism, was baptised at Lowestoft in 1567.

Giles Fletcher, the poet best known for his four canto allegorical poem 'Christ's Victory and Triumph' (1610), was rector of Alderton.

George Borrow (1803–1881) author of such novels and travelogues as *The Bible in Spain*, *Lavengro* and *The Romany Rye*, that were enormously popular in the nineteenth century, lived at Oulton Broad and died in Lowestoft.

The Reverend Cornelius Whur, who died at Bungay in 1853, is often listed among the ten worst published poets in the English Language. He genuinely cared about the sufferings of the less fortunate members of his flock, but it did not translate well into his poetry. Here is a sample:

> Alas! Alas! the father said,
> O what a dispensation!
> How can we be by mercy led,
> In such a situation?
> Be not surprised at my alarms,
> The dearest boy is without arms!

I have no hope, no confidence,
The scene around is dreary;
How can I meet such vast expense?
I am by trying weary.
You must, my dearest, plainly see
This armless boy will ruin me.

Among Whur's other works can be found such profundities as 'The Diseased Legs' and 'The Cheerful Invalid'.

Ruth Dugdall of Felixstowe was the winner of the Crime Writers' Association Debut Dagger in 2005, with her book *The Woman Before Me*.

Adrian Bell (1901–1980) was a 20-year-old, rather bohemian young man, who had gained a good education in Battersea, when he answered the call of the country life and came to Suffolk as an apprentice to Vic Savage, a yeoman farmer at Carlton Colville. Graduating to a small farm of his own, Bell went on to farm in several locations for the next sixty years, notably at Redisham where he had a smallholding of 89 acres. Drawing on his experiences of country life and work he evocatively recreated them in his best-selling farm trilogy of *Corduroy* (1930), *Silver Ley* (1931) and *The Cherry Tree* (1932), which have all been reprinted many times since. He went on to write another twenty books about the countryside and farming; he wrote the weekly 'Countryman's Notebook' column in the *Eastern Daily Press* from 1950 but it remains a little-known fact that he was also the first compiler of *The Times* crossword. Adrian's son is the former Suffolk Regiment NCO, BBC war reporter, author, independent MP and UNICEF Ambassador Martin Bell, who was born at Redisham in 1938.

Ipswich is the home of the ancestors and some living relatives of Geoffrey Chaucer (1343–1400), author of *The Canterbury Tales*.

John O'Lydgate, also known as John of Bury (*c.* 137–1451), was born at Lidgate but spent most of his life as a monk in the monastery at Bury St Edmunds. While there he wrote poetry and his output was prodigious to say the least, for it extends to at least 145,000 lines of verse and includes such tomes as his *Troy-book*, a translation of Trojan history running to 30,117 lines, and his *magnum opus,* the *Fall of Princes,* at 36,365 lines.

Allan Jobson (1889–1980) grew up in the Greater London suburb of Anerley but loved his visits to his mother's family home of Rackford Farm in Middleton, Suffolk. He bought his first home in Suffolk at Westleton shortly before the Second World War and he and his family decamped there to avoid the worst of the Blitz. Their family home in London was bombed out and was compulsorily purchased after the war. Allan decided to move permanently to Suffolk, buying a house on St George's Road, Felixstowe, where he spent the next forty years of his life until his death in 1980. Allan Jobson's books capture the very essence of Suffolk people, village life and character in the past. They are written by a man who really knew and loved the place and are effused with historical facts and snippets of interest and value to historian and casual reader alike. To this day, his books endure as some of the the most enjoyable and readable about the county, and although many are out of prints they are well worth tracking down and would make a fine collection on any Suffolk bookshelf. Allan's grandson, Richard Blake, has kindly suggested what he considers the best of Allan's books: *Suffolk Yesterdays* (1945), *This Suffolk* (1948), *North East Suffolk* (1948) and *Household and Country Crafts* (1953).

Charles Dickens (1812–1870) was a regular visitor to Suffolk. He holidayed here, visited on numerous occasions and gave some of his public readings in the county. There are frequent references to Suffolk locations in his works including Blunderston (which Dickens calls Blunderstone), where David Copperfield was born at the hall; Eatanswill in *The Pickwick Papers* is based on Sudbury; Ipswich gets a mention and Mr Pickwick himself stayed at the Angel at Bury St Edmunds.

Wilkie Collins was also inspired by his visits to Suffolk and set a scene in his novel *No Name* (1862) at Aldeburgh, which appears in his fictional version as Aldborough.

Captain Charles Hamilton Sorley (1895–1915) of the 7th (Service) Battalion, the Suffolk Regiment, was described by Robert Graves in *Goodbye to All That* as 'one of the three poets of importance killed during the war'. Sorley was killed at the Battle of Loos on 13 October 1915. His sole work *Marlborough and Other Poems* was published posthumously in January 1916.

M.R. James (1862–1936), the father of the modern ghost story, grew up at Great Livermere rectory from the age of three and set a number of his eerie tales in Suffolk – notably *Oh, Whistle, and I'll Come to You, My*

Lad in Felixstowe, *A Warning to the Curious at Aldeburgh*, and *Rats and A Vignette at Great Livermere*.

Stewart P. Evans, crime historian and author of *The Lodger: Arrest and Escape of Jack the Ripper* (1995), *Jack the Ripper: Letters from Hell* (2001), *The Ultimate Jack the Ripper Companion* (2000), *Jack the Ripper: Scotland Yard Investigates* (2010) and *Executioner: The Chronicles of James Berry, Victorian Hangman* (2005), served nearly thirty years in the Suffolk constabulary and lived in Lowestoft and Bury St Edmunds.

The Seance (2008) is a spooky novel by John Harwood that revolves around the fictional Wraxford Hall – a derelict mansion on the Suffolk coast.

Moll Flanders and *Robinson Crusoe* author Daniel Defoe also wrote A *Tour Thro' the Whole Island of Great Britain (1724–27)*, in which he described Ipswich as 'one of the most agreeable places in England'.

Robert Louis Stevenson, the author of such immortal titles as *Treasure Island* and *Dr. Jeckyll and Mr Hyde* was introduced to Sidney Colvin at Cockfield Rectory in the summer of 1873. The meeting was to be key to the future of the then unpublished Stevenson, for it was Colvin who his first introduced Stevenson to a London editor. Colvin and Stevenson remained friends; Colvin even went on to edit some of Stevenson's work, including the Edinburgh edition of his works (1894–97).

Michael Forman, prolific author and illustrator of children's books for fifty years, is best known for his autobiography *War Boy: A Country Childhood* (1989), a book which was awarded the Kate Greenaway Medal and recounts his memories as young boy in Pakefield during the Second World War.

Crime fiction author Ruth Rendell, best known for her fictional detective Inspector Wexford in books and on TV, lived for some time in Polstead. She features Suffolk in many of her novels, notably under her pen-name of Barbara Vine, including such books as *Gallowglass* (1990), which she sets in Sudbury and *A Fatal Inversion* (1987) where she used Polstead. Nayland, Orford and Aldeburgh are used for part of *No Night is Too Long* (1994), and Bury St Edmunds and its surroundings for *The Brimstone Wedding* (1995).

My New Zealand Garden by 'a Suffolk Lady', which has gone through numerous editions since it was first published in 1902, was written by Beyton-born *émigré* Emily Louisa Merielina Rogers.

Charles Montagu Doughty, author of *Travels in Arabia Deserta* (1888) which is regarded by some as one of the finest travel books written, was born at Theberton Hall in 1843.

Alan Murdie, ghost hunter, *Fortean Times* columnist, chairman of The Ghost Club and author of such books as *Haunted Bury St Edmunds* (2006), *Haunted Edinburgh* (2007) co-author of *The Cambridge Ghost Book* (2000) and the best-selling *Guide to Council Tax* (since 1999), lives in Bury St Edmunds.

A thirty-one-verse poem was published in the *Ipswich Journal* to mark the tragic death of coastguardsman James Martin, who was killed by the explosion of one of the cannon on Gun Hill in Southwold while firing a salute in honour of the Prince of Wales' Birthday on 9 November 1842.

Roger A. Freeman (1928–2005), historian and author of numerous books about the US Eighth Air Force in the Second World War, was born in Ipswich.

Ivan Bunn of Lowestoft has amassed a wealth of knowledge about ghosts, the paranormal and witchcraft in East Anglia. His first book was the pamphlet *Haunted Lowestoft* (1975), which now has another further three editions. In 1997 he co-authored *A Trial of Witches: A Seventeenth Century Witchcraft Prosecution* with Gilbert Giles, which remains the most comprehensive examination of the Lowestoft Witch Trial of Amy Denny and Rose Cullender in 1662.

Best-selling novelist Norah Lofts (1904–1983), author of *The Suffolk Trilogy* and many more besides, based a number of her stories in Baildon, a fictionalised town based on Bury St Edmunds.

Nora Acheson, author of the children's book *Up the Steps, A Tale of Old Aldeburgh* (1974), was a local doctor in the town for many years. Snooks, the dog whose sculpture is familiar to all who pass the Boating Pond on the seafront, was the beloved pet of Nora and her fellow doctor husband, Robin.

Agnes Strickland, poet and author of numerous books, including the twelve-volume *Lives of the Queens of England* (1840–1848), *Lives of the Tudor Princesses, Including Lady Jane Gray and Her Sisters* (1868), and a host of children's books, was born at Reydon Hall.

Masonic historian, adventure traveller and martial arts expert Martin Faulks wrote *Butterfly Tai Chi: Energy and Tranquility in 10 Minutes a Day* (2009) and *Becoming a Ninja Warrior* (2010) when he lived in Bungay.

Crime fiction author P.D. James has a second home in Southwold and has set a number of her novels in Suffolk.

Sarah Kirby, born at Framlingham in 1741, was the granddaughter of John Kirby, the author of the popular *Suffolk Traveller* book. Writing was in her blood and under her married name of Mrs Trimmer she wrote numerous books, including *Fabulous Histories* (1786), produced the six-volume *Sacred History* (1782–84) and founded the periodical *The Guardian of Education*.

Cecil H. Lay, author of *Sparrows and Other Poems*, *Grotesques and Arabesques*, *April's Foal* and *Samples*, was born at Aldringham in 1887.

Anna Laetitia Barbauld (1743–1825), author of numerous books, notably *Lessons for Children* (1778–9), *Hymns in Prose for Children* (1781) and the poem 'Eighteen Hundred and Eleven', lived for a number of years in Palgrave.

Elizabeth Inchbald (1753–1821) novelist, actress and dramatist, and author of such works as *The Married Man* (1789), *Lover's Vows* (1798) and *The Wise Man of the East* (1799), was born at Stanningfield.

Edward Fitzgerald (1809–1883), known to the world for his version of the *Rubaiyat of Omar Khayyam*, spent nearly all his life at Boulge and Woodbridge. Buried in Boulge churchyard, the rose which grows over his stone was raised from seed, brought by the artist William Simpson from the grave of Omar Khayyam at Nashapur, and was planted by a few friends in the name of the Omar Khayyam Club in October 1898.

Nathaniel Bacon (1592–1660), born the third son of Edward Bacon of Shrubland Hall, Puritan author of *An Historical Discovery of the Uniformity of the Government of England* (1647), was buried at Coddenham.

John Lindsey, author of the novels *The Lady and the Mule*, *Sixteen Gods*, *The Bull Calf*, and *Vicarage Party and Tenderness*, was born at Hadleigh in 1909. He also wrote *Youth in Bondage* – a satirical attack on English preparatory schools, which he published under another name.

Jon Canter, TV and radio comedy sketch writer, author of the novels *Seeds of Greatness* (2006), *A Short Gentleman* (2009) and *Worth* (2011), lives in Aldeburgh with his wife, painter Helen Napper.

The 1933 novel *Ordinary Families* by E. Arnot Robinson is the story of a young girl growing up with her family in Pin Mill.

Arthur Ransome features Pin Mill in his 'Swallows and Amazons' series of books for children, first in *We Didn't Mean to Go to Sea* (1937), and again in *Secret Water* (1939).

Actress, wit and lady of letters Joyce Grenfell loved Aldeburgh. Her letters written during her visits to the town between 1962 and 1979 were edited by Janie Hampton and published in *Letters from Aldeburgh* (2006).

Meg Rosof's moving book *What I Was* (2007) was set on the East Anglian coastline, notably where the River Ore meets the sea.

Booker Prize-winning author Penelope Fitzgerald (1916–2000), listed by *The Times* in their fifty greatest British writers since 1945, based her novel *The Bookshop* (1978) on her own experiences working in bookshop in Southwold.

Wingfield Castle was the inspiration for Godsend Castle, the home of the Mortmain family in the novel *I Capture the Castle* (1949) by Dodie Smith.

V.S. (Victor Sawdon) Pritchett, author of numerous books, including, *Marching Spain* (1928), *Blind Love and Other Stores* and his best known, *Midnight Oil* (1971), was born at Ipswich in December 1900.

Pin Mill is a setting in the *Strong Winds* trilogy of children's books (2011–12) by Julia Jones.

Ipswich was the base of operations for Russian 'illegal' agent Valeri Petrofsky in the Frederick Forsyth novel *The Fourth Protocol* (1984).

Much of the novel *Die Ringe des Saturn: Eine englische Wallfahrt* (1995), published in English in 1998 as *The Rings of Saturn: An English Pilgrimage*, by W.G. Sebald describes a walking tour that follows the Suffolk coast path. The film *Patience (After Sebald)* (2012) was based on the book.

Poet and novelist Jane Taylor (1783–1824) wrote her best-known song 'Twinkle, Twinkle, Little Star' while living on Shilling Street in Lavenham.

Notable journalist and political philosopher William Godwin (17556–1836) spent most of his youth in Debenham and lived for a number of years in Stowmarket. Moving to London, Godwin married feminist Mary Wollstonecraft and they had a daughter in 1797, who they named Mary. Sadly there were complications and Mary Wollstonecraft died ten days after giving birth to her daughter. That little girl inherited the literary talents of both her parents; she would move in a circle of remarkable literary figures and eventually became Mary Shelley and wrote *Frankenstein* (1818), one of the greatest gothic horror novels of all time and one of the earliest examples of science fiction in literature.

In his autobiographical novel *Borstal Boy* (1958), Brendan Behan recounts his imprisonment at HMP Hollesley Bay. The novel was adapted into a play and a film of the same name, released in 2000, starring Shawn Hatosy and Danny Dyer.

In the epilogue of the third volume of *A Prison Diary* (2004), Jeffrey Archer recounts his experiences at HMP Hollesley Bay after his transfer there from HMP Lincoln.

Richard Shaw, author of the best-selling diet book *Cut the Crap* (2011), wrote the book whilst living in Ipswich.

5

SUFFOLK
AT WORK

FARMING TIMES

The Suffolk Dun was a large breed of dairy cattle with a high milk yield. Bred from stock imported from Holland during the late sixteenth and early seventeenth centuries, the Suffolk Dun was then crossed with the Norfolk Red beef breed to create Norfolk and Suffolk Red Polled cattle. The name was simplified to Red Polled in 1883,

before it was finally settled as Red Poll, a good name for this excellent breed, in 1888. Red Poll were introduced to America in 1873 and are the oldest registered breed of cattle in the USA.

Suffolk sheep, the Suffolk horse and Red Poll cattle are known as the 'Suffolk Trinity' of local breeds.

At the Suffolk Sheep Society's annual show sale in 1964 a ram sold for 1,100 guineas.

Pedigree Suffolk Ram semen currently commands £25 to £30 a straw.

At present there are an estimated 70,000 sheep in Suffolk.

The Suffolk pig, otherwise known as the Small Black, is now extinct.

The traditional Suffolk scythe with its 4ft 'chine' or blade, with a snaith or shaft made of ash, alder or birch, curved into a gentle 's' shape, standing about 5ft 10in tall, was the favoured scythe among the harvestmen of the eastern counties for generations.

The Suffolk Iron or Swing Plough was the first all-iron plough. It was devised and made by blacksmith John Brand, just over the border at Lawford, Essex, in 1770.

The self-sharpening chilled cast-iron plough share, patented in 1803, was discovered accidentally by Ipswich iron founder Robert Ransome when he spilled molten iron on the foundry floor. He found that where the iron hit the floor it cooled faster, causing a harder underside than the top – this principle, when applied to the manufacture of a plough share, meant they could be made with a softer top surface than the surface underneath, and so retained a sharp cutting edge. In the 1830s the firm Ransomes were making more than eighty different types of plough. The company grew to become the largest plough and agricultural equipment manufacturer in Britain, and at one time had over 3,000 employees.

The first really efficient seed drill, known as the Suffolk Seed Drill, was developed in Peasenhall in 1800 by wheelwright James Smyth, his brother Jonathan and local farmer Robert Wardley.

Garretts of Leiston produced their first internal combustion engine ploughing tractor, known as the Crawley-Garrett Agrimotor, in 1913.

Annual Meadow Grass (*Poa annua*) is also known as Suffolk Grass.

The design of the Suffolk Long Cart, a two-wheeled non-tipping cart ideal for harvesting, is medieval.

In 1947, the oldest working farmer in England was Mr Frederick Bird, who was still working Westfield Manor Farm near Ipswich, aged 95.

The Shroff Hut was a multi-purpose shed peculiar to Suffolk. It was constructed by erecting undressed trunks then adding a flat roof made of a layer of piled brushwood overlain by thatch.

According to the 1861 census there were 43,518 agricultural labourers in Suffolk; this figure had almost halved by 1921 when a figure of 22,913 was recorded.

In 1942 there were forty-two combine harvesters in use in Suffolk; by 1968 there were nearly 3,000 on the farms of the county.

The Suffolk Wagon, distinctive because of its large wheelbase, was first introduced to the county in the late eighteenth century.

Thomas Tusser (1524–1580), the poet and farmer best known for his *Five Hundred Points of Good Husbandry*, was born in Essex but chose to farm at Cattawade in Suffolk.

Ishmael Cutter, shepherd to the Earl of Stradbroke, reared 566 lambs from 406 ewes in 1833. The following year he achieved 717 lambs from 487 ewes and was awarded the Honourary Silver Medal by the Agricultural Association in 1835.

John Chevalier of Aspall (1774–1846), Rector of Badingham, was an expert agriculturalist. The story of his greatest discovery tells of how one of his labouring parishioners, returning from threshing at Debenham, had an uncomfortable walk back, and taking off his boot discovered that an ear of barley had been the cause of his discomfort. He sowed these grains in his garden and these were noticed by Chevalier, who thought they looked good and begged an ear or two for himself. Chevalier raised enough from these to seed a field and grew what was hailed as 'The best barley yet produced'. Chevalier barley soon became world famous.

SUFFOLK PUNCH

The Suffolk horse, also known as Suffolk Sorrel, is best known as a Suffolk Punch.

The Suffolk horse was first recorded in the sixteenth century and was mentioned in William Camden's *Britannia* (1586).

The Suffolk Punch registry is the oldest English breed society.

Suffolk Punches generally stand 16.1 to 17.2 hands (65-70in/165-178cm) and weigh 1,980 to 2,200 pounds (900-1,000kg).

The Suffolk Punch is always a shade of 'chesnut' in colour, be it dark red to light – note the spelling with no 't', for it is the traditional one, still used by the Suffolk Horse Society.

Every animal of the current breed of Suffolk Punch can be traced back to a foundation sire foaled near Woodbridge in 1768 that was owned by Thomas Crisp of Ufford.

A Suffolk Punch imported to Denmark in the 1860s by noted Suffolk dealer Oppenheimer of Hamburg was one of the founding stallions of the Jutland breed.

The first Suffolks were imported to the United States in 1880; more followed in 1888 and in 1903 to begin the breeding of Suffolk Punches in the US. The American Suffolk Horse Association was established and published its first stud book in 1907. By 1908, the Suffolk had also been exported from England to Europe, Russia, Sweden, Africa, New Zealand, Australia, Argentina and many other countries.

A team of Suffolk geldings from Sudbourne that exhibited at Olympia in 1908 beat all comers, with their total weight exceeding 6 tons. After the show, this team was sold to Mr Bostock, the circus proprietor, for 1,100 guineas.

The Suffolk Punch is known as a 'good worker' with a good 'pull' for plough and other agricultural machinery. Suffolks became the main driving force on the farms of East Anglia until after the Second World War, when more and more farms could afford tractors. The breed went into decline and only nine foals were registered with the Suffolk Horse Society in 1966.

Great efforts have been made to keep the breed going. The breed remains rare but numbers have increased to eighty breeding mares in Britain, producing around forty foals per year by the mid-1990s.

The largest Suffolk Punch stud farm in the country was begun by the prison service at Hollesley Bay who ran it for over twenty years. Plans were made to sell off the prison farms and, fearing that that sale would mean the dispersal of the Colony Stud, the Suffolk Punch Trust was established in 2002 and given three years to raise the money to buy a 200-acre farm and the horses. Today, the Trust not only has the stud, but other rare Suffolk breeds such as Red Poll cattle, Large Black Pigs, Ixworth chickens and the oldest registered flock of Suffolk sheep in the world.

THE COUNTY LORE OF THE AGRICULTURAL LABOURERS' WORKING DAY

Traditionally, the labourer began work at sunup, and concluded his labours by sundown.

Every day was interspersed with breaks, otherwise described as whets or naps.

The day would start with the dew drink, often just cold tea or spring water. Few would have had a hearty breakfast – most would have regularly started their day with just bread and cheese, perhaps a boiled egg or a bit of bacon for a treat.

As the sun gets high in the sky, the labourer knew it was time for 'levenses and a good drink from the bottle of cold tea he had brought with him. This would be only a brief break and if the labourer had been standing to do his task he may well not sit down, lest he 'get stuck' (get tempted to linger too long over his break), and then go back to work until lunch time.

The lunch break was known as 'nuneins' or 'nune-time', and the workman would stop for a while and walk to a bank, probably shaded by a tree or hedge or haystack and sit down with his workmates. The real old labourers were known to chew tobacco and would take the chunk from their mouth. If bald they removed their hats, stuck the sticky chewed 'baccy' on the top of their head, put their hat back on and have their lunch. This repast would usually consist of a hunk of bread, a bit of cheese, an onion and perhaps an apple or a pear if in season, which had all been carried in his wickle-poke (lunch bag). During 'nune-time' life, country philosophy, jokes, local sports and local events would be discussed. Then off to work again for the afternoon; many of the men puffing away determinedly on their roll-up fags as they walked back.

'Fowerses' or 'Beevers' was the last break, usually at about four in the afternoon. The wife of the labourer might bring or send one of the children over ready for this break with a billycan of milk 'sop' – milk with bread 'bobs' broken into it, sometimes heated up. If it was harvest time, or the men deserved reward, the farmer might well send over a flagon of beer in a stone jar encased in a handled wicker basket.

THE SUFFOLK SHOW

The Suffolk Agricultural association was formed in 1831 and held its first show in 1832, at Wickham Market. Four years later, the West and East Suffolk Agricultural Associations amalgamated and the Suffolk Agricultural Association was formed.

The first Suffolk Show prize money amounted to a grand total of £101.

The Suffolk Agricultural Association's first president was the Earl of Stradbroke, who remained in office for fifty-five years.

The Suffolk Agricultural Association's first secretary was Mr Cornelius Welton of Wickam Market.

From its early years until 1956 the Show was held at a different location every year.

In 1956, the Suffolk Show attracted a remarkable 52,406 people.

The Suffolk Show has been held on the Bucklesham Road site, now known as Trinity Park, on the eastern outskirts of Ipswich since 1960.

By 2013 there were 375 competitive classes for livestock over 27 different breeds of cattle with prize money in the region of £70,000. There were also 325 equine classes, 2,000 horses or ponies, of which 200 were heavy horses.

The Suffolk Show ground covers 100 hectares in total, of which 40 hectares is an exhibition area.

SOME AGRICULTURAL IMPLEMENT AND MACHINERY MAKERS OF SUFFOLK

Charles Sheldrake (harrows), Wickham Skeith
Cornish & Lloyds Ltd, Risbygate, Bury St Edmunds
Harry N. Rumsby, Waveney Iron Works, Bungay
Harry Oxborrow (seed drills and horse hoes), Norton
James Smyth & Sons Ltd (corn and seed drills), Peasenhall and
    Saxmundham
Ransomes, Sims & Jeffries Ltd, Orwell Works, Ipswich
Richard Garrett & Sons, Leiston Works
Warren & Sons, Blackbourn Iron Works, Elmswell
Woods, Cocksedge and Warner of Stowmarket and Bury St Edmunds

COUNTING SHEEP

In order to keep an accurate account of births or deaths or to detect strays, shepherds performed frequent headcounts of their flocks. Rather than counting with conventional numbers as we know them today, shepherds had their own numbering system. They would vary from region to region; this one was recorded as being in use in Theberton and East Bridge during the late nineteenth century:

Unna (1)	Hater (6)
Tina (2)	Skater (7)
Wether (3)	Sara (8)
Tether (4)	Dara (9)
Pinkie (5)	Dick (10)

BRANDON FLINTS

The mining and use of knapped flints in the Brandon area can be traced back over 3,000 years, but the industry of making gun flints there dates from the late seventeenth century. Men and boys would be employed to excavate and work the flint mines. Quantities of the excavated stone were measured in 'jags', which equated to about one horse-load equal to a ton. In a six-day week a typical miner would bring about three-and-a-half jags to the surface and would expect to earn around 11 pence a jag.

Flint was not only used for firearms; it was also used in tinder boxes, and shaped flint was in demand for facing churches, buildings and walls. Working with flint took great skill that could only be achieved by practical experience, feel and eye. Many old knappers claimed they could 'read' the stone and would know exactly where to strike their blow upon the flint. Boys would often begin their hands-on work 'quartering' the flint nodules, and in doing so develop a feel for and an understanding of the stone.

The flint worker would sit on a stool wearing a sturdy white canvas apron, with a hide-covered thigh pad on his leg. Picking the stone from the jag pile in his yard, he would rest the nodule on the pad on his thigh, and holding it in place with one hand, he would set about quartering the nodule using a flint hammer. After quartering came what was regarded as the most skilful of all operations as the 'flakes' were struck off the quarters using a quartering hammer. Flaking was different to knapping – the wrist would be kept tight and strike with the 'point' of the hammer. The skill was to get the flakes to break off straight and long, the aim being to get two gun flints from each flake. A skilled flaker could produce between 5,000 and 7,000 flakes a day, while an expert could strike off as many as 10,000. The cores left after the flaking process were squared up and sold to builders, and remaining waste was put aside to provide ballast for roads and, later on, the railways.

The final process was for the 'flake' to be 'knapped' using a 'flaking hammer'. Each flake would be picked up and placed upon a small, narrow oblong anvil known as a 'spike'. The flake would then be shaped into the required gun flint turned in an anti-clockwise direction, the fourth edge being created when it was struck off the flake.

It was not as easy as it looked – the secret was keeping the hammer working at a good speed with the wrist. The workers took great pride in their work too and it was proudly claimed that every flint from Brandon, where the industry flourished, was 'good for a thousand sparks'.

Brandon flints were used in the muskets of the British Army at Waterloo. During the late nineteenth century, flint manufacturers R.J. Snare Company were still producing more than 3 million flints a year. During the first half of the twentieth century the gun flint industry died out to become a specialised craft carried out a by a few individuals, and the last of the old Brandon knappers died in the 1980s.

MADE IN SUFFOLK

In 1929 the main products of the county were recorded in Kelly's Trade Directory as: 'Cement stone [for Roman cement], lime, marl, whiting, bricks, gunflints, corn, malt, flax and cattle; the breeds of horses and pigs and some fame.' Other industries deemed worthy of mention were the herring and mackerel fisheries, artificial manures, gun cotton, bricks

and tiles. The smaller industries recorded were silk, linen, woollen horsehair seating, rugs, mats and matting, rabbit skin dressing, and coach and ship building.

WHAT'S MY LINE?

Unusual ways to earn a crust in nineteenth-century Ipswich:

P. Podd, **Bird and Animal Preserver**, St Stephen's Lane
Robert Pigg, **Fellmonger** (dealer in skins), Woodbridge Road
James Hazell, **Horse Clipper**, Black Horse Lane
George King, **Mill Band Manufacturer**, Princes Street
M. Marshall, **Sawmaker**, Upper Orwell Street
Henry Churchman, **Snuff Manufacturer**, Hyde Park Corner
Joshua and Cornelius Clarke, **Soap Manufacturers**, Greyfriars Road
Ebenezer Goddard, **Naptha, Creosote & Cart Grease Manufacturer**,
   Asphalte Works, Bramford
Charles Sullings, **Brush Maker**, St Stephen's Lane
Thomas Smith, **Coach Spring Maker**, Black Horse Lane
David Holland, **Clog and Pattern Maker**, College Street
Aaron Bell, **Cork Manufacturer**, High Street
Mrs R. Fayers, **Straw Bonnet Maker**, Norwich Road
John Oxford, **Trussmaker**, Market Lane
James Goodwin, **Tobacco Pipe Manufacturer**, Fore Street

TOUCHING CLOTH

Suffolk Hempen Cloth was once a well-regarded textile produced by weavers across the county. Silk, serge and baize were also produced here to the degree, and a significant number people found employment in the manufacture of these stuffs during the eighteenth and up to the early nineteenth century, when most of these cottage industries moved away from the county to the new factories of the industrial north.

Haverhill had been a noted centre for the manufacture of smocks made from a hard-wearing, coarse, linen-like material known as Drabbett. D. Gurteen & Sons had been in the town since the 1780s did not desert Haverhill; instead they built a factory in 1856, and by 1900 the Gurteen Company employed over 2,500 personnel. It is still manufacturing quality clothing in the town today.

SUGAR FIRST

The very first sugar beet factory in Britain was begun at Lavenham in 1868 by Mr James Duncan and completed in February 1869. Duncan had made agreements with local farmers in the neighbourhood to grow beet for him at the price of 20s per ton of clean roots, delivered at his factory. Sadly, the local farmers could not be persuaded to grow this new crop in sufficient quantity for the business to be viable, so it closed in the 1870s.

SUFFOLK TRADES AND BUSINESSES

In 1861 there were over 6,000 people employed in the boot and shoe craft and industries – this had fallen to less than 1,000 by 1931.

In 1951 there were sixty-three practicing master house thatchers in Suffolk.

Between 1851 and 1901 the number of people employed on the railways in Suffolk (excluding construction) increased eight-fold from 251 people to 2,035.

In 1851 there were eleven children aged between 10 and 14 employed as chimney sweeps in the county.

During the nineteenth century, Eye had a fine reputation for producing pillow lace.

According to the 1891 census there were 2,024 blacksmiths in Suffolk.

An ink factory existed at Barsham near Beccles in the late nineteenth century.

Nursey of Bungay have been making sheepskin garments since 1846.

Birds Eye frozen foods has been located in Lowestoft for over sixty years, and remains a major employer with some 700 workers.

During the second half of the eighteenth century, a factory on Crown Street in Lowestoft produced soft-paste porcelain ware. Today, Lowestoft porcelain is a rare and highly collectable antique.

United Automobile Services was founded in Lowestoft in 1912 to run the local bus services and began a coach-building business in 1920. Hived off to Eastern Counties Omnibus Company in 1931, the coachworks were separated into a new company – Eastern Coach Works – which grew to become the largest full-time employer in the town.

A beatster was the name given to the women and girls who repaired the fishing nets at Lowestoft.

A 'thakker' is a Suffolk word for a thatcher.

HERRING HEYDAYS

Shoals of herring were known affectionately as 'silver darlings'.

Agricultural labourers who were low on work out of harvest time would walk to the fishing ports to find work. Sometimes, this journey would take several days and the men who slept rough in any available green cover while on this journey, and who rose again with the sun, were known as 'hedge sparrows' or 'joskins'.

The standard crew of a drifter would consist of ten men – the skipper, mate, oarsman (hawseman), net ropeman, cast off, driver (engineer), assistant engineer (stoker), deck hands and a cook.

Drifters steamed out in daylight so they could cast their nets at night when the herring were pursuing plankton to feed and 'swimming at their best'.

Drifters got their name from their nets which they cast and allowed to drift with the tide.

Each net was 39ft deep by 105ft long. The nets shot varied in number between 81 and 101 (but folklore dictated there should always be an odd number) and thus could stretch as far away as 2 miles.

Trawlers went to sea for anywhere up to ten days, while drifters aimed to put into port every morning with a fresh catch. If the catch was poor the skipper would usually decide to stay out another night in hopes of obtaining a better haul.

A large, heavy catch could take up to fourteen hours to be hauled in by hand.

Once the herrings had been taken off the boat, the catch was stored in the hold. The nets would then need to be cleaned and stored above the catch – failure to do this job properly could cause the hemp of the net to react with the fish oil and spontaneously combust!

Once a boat reached port, a sample of its catch was rushed to the sale ring and buyers would base their price on this. The same sample would also be retained until unloading was completed in case of dispute.

Some large catches could take ten to twelve hours to unload from boat to quayside.

The cran was the official measure for herring and was equivalent to 26-28 stones or 37.5 gallons. There were roughly 1,000 to 1,200 fish in a cran.

The cran was made a legal measure in England and Wales in 1908.

In Lowestoft, the basket in general use held a quarter of a cran, the construction of which was regulated by law: 'The Quarter-Cran, showing the raised centre, the branded piece of hardwood beneath each cane handle, 1½ inches broad, &c.; pieces of hoopwood (6 in number), 1 inch broad, bark outermost and equi-distant with willows in between; also the binding, waling and cane fitching, according to precise instructions issued by the Fishery Board.'

Two hundred crans of herring was regarded as 'a good catch' for any boat.

The biggest recorded catch at Lowestoft was 310 crans, caught by the Lowestoft drifter *Reward* on 14 October 1913.

In 1913, Lowestoft had 350 English and 420 Scottish boats that landed almost 535,000 crans.

In 1948 1,706 seamen were employed at Lowestoft.

In 1949, Lowestoft had 78 Scotch boats and 44 local fishing boats that landed 296,194 crans, or more than 180 million fish, worth £651,142. In that same year the 'top boat' in Lowestoft made the princely sum of £9,333, while some of the smaller boats made as little as £500.

Each spring, the more seaworthy boats of the East Anglian fishing fleets moved north to 'follow the herring' and to take part in the Scotch voyage.

During the herring boom of 1907, 2.5 million barrels of fish (250,000 tons) were cured and exported from Great Yarmouth and Lowestoft, the main markets at the time being North Germany, Eastern Europe and Russia.

In 1912 there were a total of 2,136 coopers and 10,818 gutters and packers employed in the East Coast herring industry.

The last major Lowestoft herring fishers, Small & Co., phased out catching herring in 1966, and the remains of the herring fleet petered out by 1970.

6

SENSE OF PLACE

SYLLY SUFFOLK

On hearing the term Sylly Suffolk, many people assume that it refers to the ancient inhabitants of the county being silly rather than its true meaning, which is 'Holy'. They are, however, not entirely wrong because the fair county of Suffolk produced at least three renowned court jesters. In Camden's *Britannia*, reference is made to Baldwin le Petteur who held lands at Hemingstone 'by the ridiculous serjeantcy of Jumping, belching and farting before the king'. At Wattisham, the Wachesham family held the Manor in the reigns of Edward I, II and III 'by the same indecent service as that at Hemingstone'. Probably best known of the court jesters from Suffolk was John Scogan, a native of Bury St Edmunds and jester to Edward IV. His jests were well collected in the sixteenth century. One which has passed down through time describes when he was given his great house at Bury, near St Mary's Church. His noble-born wife stated she would not be able to find her way to church without a page. 'Poor lass!' cried Scogan. 'You shall have a guide to church before the bells ring tomorrow morning.' The Jester rose early and had a chalk line drawn from his house to the church. When the time came to go to church, he opened the house door and with a flourish of his hand towards the chalk line, proclaimed 'There be your guide!' The fastidious lady 'waxed so wrath at the practical trick played by her husband, that all his wit could hardly pacify her'.

THE ROARING BOYS OF PAKEFIELD

In 1888, the Rector of Pakefield publicly defended his stance on criticising the Mayor of Lowestoft holding a New Year Ball, on the grounds of dancing for entertainment being evil. Perhaps he had heard the old poem:

The roaring boys of Pakefield,
Oh, how they all do thrive!
They had but one poor parson
And him they buried alive.

THE TALE OF SHELLEY COOK

'Shelley' Cook was a 3ft dwarf and well-known Lowestoft character, who was often put in the cells of the local police station to sleep of his state of intoxication. This was not really through his personal spending on drink but rather, he was fed drinks until helplessly drunk for the sport and amusement of local 'wags'. His plight was noticed by well-meaning local 'blue ribboners' – teetotal folk who guided him away from those who would lead him astray. One evening, while on his way to chapel, his bible tucked under his arm, he bumped into a group of his old 'friends' and was led astray to a number of the local hostelries. Shelley was absolutely 'bladdered' by the time he was transported back to his sister's house in a wheelbarrow and unceremoniously tipped out on the kitchen floor to sleep it off. Tragically, Shelley didn't wake up in the morning – he was 65. Given a very fine and well-attended funeral, one can't help but think he would have enjoyed the thought of the inquest into his death being held at the Fox and Hounds Inn.

A FREE SCHOOL

Summerhill, the unique independent boarding school founded by Alexander Sutherland Neill in 1921, is located in Leiston. The school is run as a democracy where students and staff all have an equal vote. The school's ethos is based upon the belief that school should be made to fit the child, not the other way around, and members of the school are free to do as they please, as long as their actions do not cause harm to others. As Neill would say, the principle is 'Freedom, not License'.

BIG BANG

The most catastrophic event ever to occur in Stowmarket was the two explosions that occurred at Prentice's Gun Cotton Factory on 11 August 1871. Twenty-eight people died, and reports of damage to windows caused by the blast were recorded for several miles around the town.

WIFE SELLING

In January 1787, the *Ipswich Journal* published the following, without any remark of it being an unusual occurrence: 'A farmer of the parish of Stowupland sold his wife to a neighbour for five guineas, and being happy to think he had made a good bargain, presented her with a guinea to buy her a new gown; he then went to Stowmarket, and gave orders for the bells to be rung upon the occasion.'

BURY FAIR

Bury Autumn Fair was in existence for about 600 years. Usually commencing around the second week in October, the fair had been colloquially known as the 'marriage market' for years. In 1802, fourteen constables received 5s each for keeping order at the fair, following

increasing complaints about the visitors' bawdy and raucous nature. John Glyde Jnr commented that the fair's great attractions were petty shows, roundabouts, gingerbread stalls and toys; 'It is a perfect nuisance to the respectable inhabitants of the town.' By the early nineteenth century, the fair took a month to set up, lasted for about four weeks and took a week to take down and clear up, and the local traders really had had enough. Bury Fair was finally abolished in 1871.

THE OLD FAIRS OF SUFFOLK

(Recorded as still extant in 1861)

Aldeburgh – 1 March, 3 May
Aldringham – 11 October, 1 December
Barrow – 1 May
Beccles – Whit Monday, 19 June, 2 October
Bergholt – 19 July
Bergholt (East) – Last Wednesday and Thursday in July
Bildeston – Ash Wednesday, Holy Thursday
Blythborough – 5 April
Botesdale – Holy Thursday
Boxford – Easter Monday, 21 December
Boxted – Whit Tuesday
Brandon – 14 February, 11 June, 11 November
Bricet – 5 July
Bungay – 14 May, 25 September
Bures – Holy Thursday
Bury St Edmunds – Easter Tuesday, 2 October, 1 December
Cavendish – 11 June
Clare – Easter Tuesday
Cold – 11 and 12 December
Cooling – 31 July, 17 October
Debenham – 24 June
Dunwich – 25 July
Dunningworth – 11 August
Elmset – Whit Tuesday
Earl Soham – 23 July
Eye – Whit Monday
Felsham – 16 August
Finningham – 4 September
Framlingham – Whit Monday, 11 October
Framsden – Holy Thursday

Glemsford – 24 June

Great Thurlow – 10 October

Hadleigh – Whit Monday, 22 September

Hacheston – 13 November

Halesworth – 29 October

Haughley – 25 August

Haverhill – 12 May, 26 August

Hinton – 22 June

Horringer – 4 September

Hoxne – 1 December, for chapmen

Hundon – Holy Thursday

Ipswich – First Tuesday in May, 22 August for lambs

Kedington – 29 June

Kersey – Easter Monday

Lavenham – Shrove Tuesday, 10 October

Laxfield – 12 May, 10 October

Lindsey – 15 July

Lowestoft – 12 May, 10 October

Market Weston – 15 August

Melford – Whit Tuesday

Melton – Second Tuesday in September for lambs, Wednesday week after Michaelmas day for cattle

Mendlesham – Holy Thursday

Mildenhall – 10 October

Nayland – 2 October

Needham – 12 and 13 October

Newmarket – Whit Tuesday, 8 November

Orford – 24 June

Polstead – 16 June

Saxmundham – Holy Thursday, 10 August, 18 August for lambs

Snape – 11 August for horses

Southwold – Trinity Monday, 25 August

Stanton – Whit Monday

Stoke – 25 February, Whit Monday, 12 May

Stowmarket – 10 July, 12 August

Stradbroke – 21 September, 12 August

Stratford – 11 June

Sudbury – 12 March, 10 July, 4 September

Thrandiston – 31 July

Thwaite – 30 June, 26 November

Woodbridge – First Tuesday in April for cattle, horses etc., 2 and 3 October for toys, 12 October

Woolpit – 16 September for horses, 19 September for cattle and toys

SOME OF THE OLD GENTRY
NAMES OF SUFFOLK

Appleyard of Waldringfield
Aylmer of Claydon
Bacon of Redgrave
Barnardiston of Barnardiston
Bedingfield of Darsham
Blois of Cockfield
Blosse of Belstead
Bowtell of Parham
Brooke of Aspall and Ufford
Cadogans of Culford
Chevallier of Aspall Hall
Clench of Creeting Hall
Clopton of Long Melford
Copinger of Buxhall
Crofts of Saxham
Darcy of Kentwell Hall
De la Pole, Dukes of Suffolk
Elwes of Stoke-juxta Clare
Felton of Playford
Ffolkes of Hillington
Gage of Hengrave
Gawdy of Crows Hall, Debenham
Gooch of Benacre
Gosnold of Otley
Grafton of Euston
Hervey of Ickworth
Higham of Hunston Hall
Hovell of Rickinghall
Jenney of Knodishall
Keble of Stowupland
Parker of Erwarton
Poley of Badley Hall and Bury
Meadows of Witnesham
Stradbroke of Henham
Sulyard of Wetherden
Talmache of Bentley and Helmingham
Tyrell of Gipping
Waldegrave of Bures

SOME UNFORTUNATE SUFFOLK SURNAMES

(All are quite genuine, and are recorded on the nineteenth-century census returns)

Billy Bastard (Bury St Edmunds, 1881)
Florasbell Bender (Long Melford, 1889)
Lavinia Bent (Bungay, 1854)
Charles Sneezum (East Bergholt, 1852)
John Boghurst (Ipswich, 1861)
Augustus Bollock (Ipswich 1881)
Mary Bottom (Earsham 1876)
Benjamin Botty (Syleham, 1841)
Emma Bugg (Trimley St Mary, 1891)
Philip Bummer (Darsham, 1861)
Hezakiah Bush (Wortham, 1836)
Mary Buttock (Cavendish, Suffolk)
John Crack (Livermere, 1826)
Emma Crapman (Lawshall 1873)
Kate Crapper (Ipswich, 1871)
Arthur Crapwell (Grundisburgh, 1862)
Willy Crotch (Woodbridge 1811)
David Cunt (Wickhambrook, 1861)
Fanny Death (Stowlangtoft, 1801)
Alice Dung (Felsham, 1824)

Belinda Dunger (Eye, 1880)
Absolom Feavearyear (Laxfield, 1858)
Ellen Frigg (Assington, Suffolk)
Leah Grope (Woodbridge 1831)
Maria Gussett (Bures 1825)
William Maggot (Eye, 1838)
Fred Papper (Otley 1872)
Charlie Papps (Nayland, 1872)
Mary Prick (Bury St Edmunds, 1814)
Isabella Prig (Wickhambrook, 1829)
Margaret Puke (Onehouse, Suffolk)
Rhoda Rotter (Stilton, 1835)
Ann Rose Shitter (Bramford, 1851)
Mary Ann Spittle (Hadleigh, 1842)
Willy Spunk (Combs, 1881)
Gertrude Stick (Stowmarket, 1871)
Tampion Cunnell (Athelington, 1894)
Jimmy Sucker (Ilketshall St Lawrence, 1871)
Jacob Wang (Bacton 1831)
Eliza Wart (Lavenham 1871)
Jack Worm (Earsham, 1856)

WELL, FANCY THAT!

Leiston Abbey ruins and farm was bought in 1928 by Miss Ellen Wrightson for use as a religious retreat. When she died in 1946, she bequeathed the house, ruins, land and buildings to the Diocese of St Edmundsbury and Ipswich.

The county flower of Suffolk is the oxlip.

Lowestoft lifeboat station is the oldest in the county and is one of the oldest in the British Isles.

The old motto of East Suffolk, granted in 1935, was *Opus Nostrum Dirige* (Direct Our Work). It was adopted by Suffolk County Council who applied their translation to it of 'Guide Our Endeavour'.

A sea serpent estimated to be some 60ft long was sighted by Lilias Rider Haggard, daughter of the great author H. Rider Haggard at Kessingland in July 1912. Her story was confirmed by her cook and her gardener, who also saw the creature.

In 1878, Ashbocking vicarage was recorded as one of the driest places in England, having received just 19in of rainfall all year.

Around the year 1800, peregrine falcons would annually nest in the steeple of Corton Church.

There are 154 remaining medieval rood screens, 14 medieval fonts and 14 pre-Reformation pulpits to be found in Suffolk churches.

Of the Suffolk churches, 126 still have their old scratch dials.

In 1901, the badger had become so seldom seen in Suffolk that enquires were made, via the press, if any were known to have bred in the county in the previous fifty years.

Gorleston was officially part of Suffolk until it merged with Great Yarmouth in 1835.

A 'Death Cafe' was held in Bury St Edmunds in April, May and June in 2013. The aim of the events, according to their publicity, was for people to 'come together in a relaxed and safe setting to discuss life and death, drink tea and eat delicious cake'.

Lowestoft's narrow lanes with steps running steeply towards the sea are known as 'scores'.

Pleasurewood Hills was created by entrepreneur Joe Larter as a small American-themed family attraction in 1983.

The manuscripts of Sir Nicholas L'Estrange of Hunstanton Hall, who died in 1669, records: 'The Bury Ladyes that us'd hawking and hunting were once in a great vaine of wearing breeches.'

Influential artist Francis Bacon (1902–1992) would often attend riotous parties staged at Westgate House in Long Melford, the home of his lover's brother, David Edwards.

Wallis Simpson stayed at Beach House, Felixstowe, during the abdication crisis in 1936, and also while her divorce was being heard in Ipswich to establish a residential qualification to allow her to marry the uncrowned King Edward VIII.

Drinkstone Mill (1689) is the oldest surviving post mill in Suffolk.

There has been a tide mill working on the same site at Woodbridge for over 800 years. In 1957 it became the last working tide mill to close. Restored and opened to the public in 1973, it remains a living museum to this day.

The Nutshell pub in Bury St Edmunds is one of the smallest pubs in England.

In 1819, the Theatre Royal at Bury St Edmunds was built by William Wilkins, who was also the architect for the National Gallery.

Ipswich Transport Museum has the largest collection of transport items devoted to one town in Britain.

Moyse's Hall Museum, built around 1180, is one of the oldest domestic buildings in East Anglia that is open to the public.

Britain's heaviest baby girl was born at the Ipswich Hospital on 20 February 2012, weighing 14lb 4oz.

According to the 1951 census, 42,529 (32.1 per cent) of households in Suffolk did not have an inside toilet. In 1971 there were still over 7,000 homes in the county where people had to use the little house down the garden.

In the 1850s and '60s one of the most unusual competitions was held annually at the Suffolk Show – one for the agricultural labourer with the largest family and who needed the least assistance from the Parish Council. One winner in 1860 mustered eighteen children and his sole call on the council was for £5 17s 6d sickness relief.

The 'Big Bury Piss Up', held annually on the first Friday of November, is supposedly to remember 'Big Beer Barry', a townsman that drank himself to death on Greene King IPA on the first Friday of November 1973.

Finnish rock band Absoluuttinen Nollapiste have a song called 'Ipswich' on their 2002 album *Nimi Muutettu*.

The last Abbot of Bury St Edmunds was John Reeve, alias Melford, a native of Melford, who was elected in 1514. Abbot Reeve surrendered the abbey and its possessions to the King in November 1539, and on doing this an annuity of 500 marks was conferred upon him. He retired to a large house that stood at the south-west corner of Crown Street, and died less than a year later on 31 March 1540.

The Gothic lantern tower of St Edmundsbury Cathedral, begun in 2000 and opened in 2005, is 150ft (45m) tall. A painted and gilded vault was unveiled under the tower in 2010.

The first internet bench (where people could connect laptops to the internet) was installed in the Abbey Gardens at Bury St Edmunds in 2001.

The Suffolk Pink, so distinctive to the cottages and farmhouses of the county, was made by blending pig or ox blood along with sloe berries or red ochre (derived from iron which really gave it its pink colour) with whitewash.

The Suffolk Latch emerged as a distinctive type of door furniture in the sixteenth century.

A Suffolk Stile is in fact a ditch dug by Suffolk farmers to mark a field enclosure.

According to Charles W. Bardsley's *A Dictionary of English and Welsh Surnames* (1901), the first recorded use of Suffolk as a surname was that of Thomas Saffauk in London in 1273. It was used to denote someone from the county, thus was only given to those who had moved away from the county.

The formal title Earl of East Anglia was created after the Norman Conquest and was often referred to as the Earl of Norfolk and Suffolk. The first man to be granted the title was Radulf Stalre in 1069. The title did not exist for long, for Ralph de Gael, the second Earl, participated in the Revolt of the Earls in 1075 – the revolt failed and the title was forfeited.

Suffolk white bricks, also known as Woolpit white bricks, are made from the Gault or Boulder clay found in the area around the village of Woolpit.

The first man to hold the single title of Earl of Suffolk was Robert d'Ufford, who was granted it in 1069.

The Suffolk Knot is a particular method of tying a rope or line. It was so named because it was used as a badge in the heraldry of John de la Pole, 2nd Duke of Suffolk (1442–1492).

The Suffolk Rose – or to call it by its botanical name, Rose Suffolk – was first recorded in 1988.

Ransome's of Ipswich produced one of the first hand-powered lawnmowers known as the Automaton in 1867. Selling upwards of 1,000 units in the first season of production, it came in a variety of sizes. The smallest machine suitable for small lawns was priced at £2 15*s*, while to a horse-drawn variant with a 16in cutting width for really big gardens was offered for £24. Ransome's went on to produce the first commercially available internal combustion engine lawnmower in 1902.

The Suffolk Punch lawnmower was first produced by Suffolk Lawn Mowers at the Suffolk Iron Foundaries at Stowmarket in 1954.

The Suffolk Puff, or Yo-Yo, is a small circle of fabric traditionally used in patchwork and quilting.

Suffolk Fairmaids, a complimentary term given to the beauty of the women of the county, is an old one and can be found in a number of texts, such as the Elizabethan play *The Honourable History of Friar Bacon*

and Friar Bungay, written by Robert Greene. The play includes the lines, when describing Margaret the Fairmaid of Fressingfield:

> A bonnier wench all Suffolk cannot yield.
> All Suffolk! Nay, all England holds none such.

THE BELLS! THE BELLS!

The bells of East Bergholt hang beside St Mary's Church in a bell cage. They have hung in the cage since 1531, after the money to build a bell tower disappeared with the fall of Cardinal Wolsey the previous year. The bells themselves are notable for two particular reasons: the bells themselves are also exceptional as they are believed to be the heaviest five (A, G, F#, E, and D) that are rung in England today, with a total weight of 4.75 tons. They are not rung from below by ropes attached to wheels, as is usual in change ringing; instead, the headstock is manipulated by hand by ringers standing beside the bells.

LAST MAN STANDING

When 38-year-old Jacob Foster of Dunwich died on 12 March 1790, he was buried in All Saints churchyard. His kin probably never considered his grave would take on greater significance over 200 years after his death but significant it is, as the churchyard and even the church have eroded away by time and have now disappeared over the cliffs. All Saints was the last of the six churches, three chapels, two monasteries and hundreds of gravestones and memorials which stood in old Dunwich. Thus Jacob Fosters' grave exists as the last marked grave of the original churchyards of old Dunwich; a silent sentinel and memorial to the inhabitants of the past.

PRIDE OF THE ORGANS

The most notable of the old organs of East Anglia is the instrument in Framlingham Church. The case is believed to date from about 1580 and was at one time in the chapel at Pembroke College, Cambridge. When the college wanted a larger and more up-to-date organ, Thomas Thamer of Peterborough built a new instrument into the old case in 1674, and in 1707 the organ was brought to Framlingham.

THE GENEROSITY OF DUNWICH

The early seventeenth-century account book of the Dunwich Bailiffs record the following gifts of 'shipbroken' and distressed people who passed through their parish:

1598 To a poore soldiour that came from the Emperours wares in Hungarye – six pennies.

1604 To a Scotchman which lost his ship loden with wyne – six pennies

1610 To a maimed saylor that cam out of the Turkes galleis – six pennies

1618 Geven to a travailour that was taken in Turkye and had his tong cut out of his head and maimed – eight pennies

1629 To a poore man whose leg was shott off – six pennies

1629 To one whose tongue was cut out – six pennies

1634 To a merchants wife that had great losses by the Turkes and her husband in slaverye – one shilling

1638 To a Germayne that came out of the Palatianate cuntrye – one shilling

PATRONS TAKE NOTE!

An old notice displayed up to the 1950s at the Crown Inn, Westleton, announced:

A man is specially engaged on the premises to do all the shouting, cursing and swearing that is required in this establishment. A dog is also kept to do all the barking. Our fighting man or chucker-out, has won seventy-five prize fights, has never been beaten and is a splendid shot with a revolver. An undertaker calls here every morning for orders.

CONFETTI

One of the earliest uses of coloured confetti instead of the traditional rice in the county was recorded in the *Suffolk Chronicle* in January 1897, when an account of a local wedding stated that as the bride and groom were leaving the bridesmaids took the opportunity 'to scatter over their heads as they departure clouds of tiny coloured wafers with which they had had provided themselves – a very pretty idea and one having the charm of novelty'.

SOME OF THE CLUBS AND SOCIETIES EXTANT IN IPSWICH 100 YEARS AGO

Piscatorial Ramblers
Citizens' Passive Resistance League
Independent Order of Rechabites
Working Girls Club and Restaurant
Early Closing Association
Manchester Unity Independent Order of Odd Fellows
Ancient Order of Shepherds
Society for Promoting Christianity Among the Jews
Teachers' Field Club
Licensing Laws Vigilance Society
Licensed Victuallers Protection Society
Gardeners' and Amateurs Mutual Improvement Association
Sons of Temperance
Meat Traders Association
Primrose League
Shipwrecked Seamen's Society
St. Clement's Self Help Society
Free Church Girl's Guild
London and Eastern Protestant Club
Gipping Angling Preservation Society
Unicorn Brewery Tenant's Protection Society
Boy's Life Brigade
Society for the Engagement of Industry
Suffolk Sheep Society
East Suffolk Auxiliary Bible Society
Large Black Pig Society
Eastern Counties Gas Managers Association

SOME SUFFOLK WORDS AND PHRASES

(Please note: these are colloquialisms, the written spelling of these words may vary across the county)

Absy – a sore or angry boil
Acrost – across
Affernune – afternoon
Badd – a beard
Barnt ef a wull – 'I'll be burnt if I will'
Betty – to waste time

Biggen – to make bigger
Bishy-Barnibee – a ladybird
Blackbird with two legs – a thief
Black-dark – very dark
Blow-broth – a busy-body
Bobbery – a squabble, or to make a fuss
Bobjolly – a muddle
Botty – to be stuck up
Brick-fricker – a brickmaker
Broad-best – best clothes
Buffle up – to wrap up
Bullock – to bully
Bultin – throbbing pain
Canker – a red field poppy
Canker-fret – verdigris
Cart – to carry about
Clackbox – mouth
Clash-ma-dang – swearing
Cobble – a fruit stone
Cobweb Morning – misty morning
Cock-brumble – a blackberry bush
Cooshies – sweets
Cow-tongued – kind and smooth words one minute, rough the next
Cruckle – to yield under a heavy burden
Dabbly – wet
Dardledumdue – a person without energy or desire to work
Dear me! Sars o' mine – an exclamation of surprise
Dilvered out – tired out
Doe-dangles – hardened dung pellets hanging from a sheep
Draant – to drawl
Dringling about – loitering with nothing to do
Dudder – to shake or vibrate
Fang – to catch hold of
Flop – cow dung on a pasture
Foky – spongy, as in 'a foky tarnip'
Frack – crowded
Frampled – wrinkled
Frawry – stale, bad smelling
Frawn – frozen
Frimicate – to mince one's words
Full o' know – a village oracle
Gelver – to throb
Hicken – kite; hop-scotch

Hidsirrag – a pushy person
Hog – over-high-leapfrog
Hully – very, as in 'he wor hully drunk'
Honker-donks – big, ugly feet
Hoppity-poise – hesitating
Howd – hold on, or stop
Hudderin – big for one's age, as in 'ha be a grat huddering fulla'
Hutkin – a covering for a sore finger
Julk – a hard blow or jolt
Latch – to land on
Little an' much – off and on, as in 'it ha' bin rainin' little an' much'
Loke – a bye road, private road in the country or a lane in a town or village
Loblolly – a badly cooked dish, 'neither sweet, sour, nor good'
Malahack – to cut clumsily
Mardle – to gossip
Meddle-maker – a busybody
Mole-country – graveyard
Mopsy-Wopsy – intoxicated
Mud-barges – thick books
Nannocking – idling
Nuddling – stooping
Phiz-gif – a wizened old woman
Pingler – a picky eater
Pramiskus – by chance
Pudding-pye doll – toad in the hole
Rafty – raw, damp weather

Ringled – married
Sad-bad – very ill
Roger's blast – a sudden whirlwind
Sarnick – a small quantity or distance
Sauzles – a cooked mixture of herbs and vegetables
Scaffle – a garden hoe
Scranch – to drag and make a grating or screeching noise
Scrindle – to shrivel
Scuting – three-cornered
Sheep's trattlings – sheep dung
Sights – spectacles
Sloightly on th' huh – something not quite straight, as in 'that
  picture's sloightly on th' huh'
Sneerchap – a sarcastic person
Snizzler – to blow one's nose
Sorshan – awry, aslant
Spuffle – to fly about pretending to be busy
Strome – to move about listlessly
Swacken – big and awkward
Swobble – to spill over
Tissick – an irritating cough
To ride a black horse white – to hurry violently
Trossen – thrashing wheat or barley
Twiddle – a small pimple
Weddiners – a newly married couple
Why-whiffles – fidgets, as in 'he can't kip still; he got the why-whiffles'
Wishly – to want or desire something
Wem – a defect or a worn place in a garment
Wrastle – to poke a fire

SUFFOLK PLACES AND THE OLD SUFFOLK WAYS OF PRONOUNCING THEM

Aldeburgh – Orld-bruh
Barham – Bar'um
Benacre – Benna'kh
Benhall – Bennil
Blythburgh – Blybra
Bramford – Bram'fd
Burgh – Bath or Berg
Bruisyard – Bridjit
Cavenham – Kav'nm

Chediston – Chaston
Combs – Cooms
Covehithe – Cothie
Cretingham – Cret'num
Culpho – Cuttfer
Debach – Debbidge
Dunningworth – Dunnafer
East Bergholt – Barfel
Ellough – Ell'ow

Erwarton – Arwarton
Eyke – Aik
Framlingham – Framminan
Freckenham – Freck'nm
Gisleham – Gizzling'hm
Groton – Grow'tn
Grundisburgh – Grundsburra
Halesworth – Haulsa
Heveningham – Henninham
Hollesley – Hozeley
Holton – Hoton
Homersfield – Hummus feeld
Hoxne – Hoxun
Ipswich – Ipsey or Ipsitch
Kesgrave – Kesgruv
Lawshall – Lorshaw
Lowesoft – Lastoff, Laystiff
  or Lowerstuff
Parham – Parrum

Petthaugh – Petter
Ramsholt – Ramsault
Monewden – Mulladen
Sproughton– Sprorton
Stowmarket – St'market
  or Stoomarket
Redisham – Retsam
Southwold – Sowle or Sole
Sotterley – Satterley
Sotherton – Surriton
Spexhall – Spexle
Ubbeston – Ubson
Uggeshall – Outshall or Uggash'l
Walberswick – Walsawig
Waldringfield – Wanaful
Walpole – Warple or Wapple
Wenhaston – Wennerst'n
Westhall – Westill
Yoxford – Yoxer

7

CRIME AND PUNISHMENT

DICK TURPIN IN BUNGAY

During the winter of 1739 the notorious highwayman Dick Turpin and his partner in crime, Tom King, had ridden up from London and were staying in Bungay, where they saw two young ladies receive £14 for corn. Turpin resolved to relieve them of it, but King remonstrated with the old scallywag, saying it was a pity to take the money from such pretty girls. But the horrible, pockmarked little man that was the real Dick Turpin persisted and took the girls for all they had. Turpin eventually ended up killing King by mistake while trying to evade capture, but captured he was. Turpin was executed at York as a highwayman, horse-stealer and murderer on 10 April 1739.

THE GENTLEMAN AND
WOMAN OF THE ROAD

Margaret Matthews was the daughter of a Lavenham swordmaker. The trade of her father's calling being totally unsuitable for a lady, she teamed up with Thomas Rumbold and together they terrorised the roads of Suffolk and Essex as highwaymen. Retiring on her illicit earnings, Margaret spent her late years in Norwich where she eventually died from dropsy in 1688. Rumbold kept up his life of robbery, deceptions, and cheating until the law eventually caught up with him and he was hanged at Tyburn in 1689.

THREE MARTYRS AT BECCLES

Thomas Spicer of Winston, John Deny and Edmund Poole both of Mendlesham were all burnt at Beccles on 21 May 1556. The case of 19-year-old Spicer was particularly tragic. He had been arrested by Sir John Tyrell of Gipping for failing to turn up at Mass and was thrown into Eye Gaol, where he awaited his fate with Deny and Poole. When the fateful day came at Beccles a contemporary account recorded: 'When the rose from prayer, they all went joyfullie to the stake, and being bound thereto, and the fire burning about them, they praised god in such an audible voice, it was wonderful to all.' Well, wonderful to most – a citizen of Beccles named Robert Bacon took exception and 'willed the tormonors to throwe on faggots to stop the knaves' breaths, as he termed them; so hot was his charitie.'

JOHN NOYES THE MARTYR OF LAXFIELD

Another of 'Bloody' Queen Mary I's victims, John Noyes and a few confederates met in secret to worship the Church of England rather than the Catholic Church. Witnessed in his activities and surprised at his back door, Noyes was challenged by Thomas Lovell, Chief Constable of the Hoxne Hundred, Nicholas Stannard and Wolfren Dowsing – men described as 'faithful and catholick Christians'. Arrested by Laxfield parish constables John Jacob and William Stannard, who just happened to be nearby, Noyes was thrown into Eye Gaol and then carted to Norwich to stand trial for heresy before the Bishop of Norwich. Found guilty, he was sentenced to be burned at the stake at Lawfield on 22 September 1557, an occasion that drew a great crowd. His final words were against the idolatry of Catholics:

'They say they can make God of a piece of bread, believe them not!' *Foxes' Book of Martyrs* concludes of the event: 'And so he yielded up his life, and when his body was burned, they made a pit to bury the coals and ashes, and amongst the same they found one of his feet that was unburned, whole up to the ankle, with the hose on, and that they buried with the rest.'

THE IPSWICH MARTYRS

The Ipswich Martyrs were nine people from, judged or burnt at the stake in the town for their Protestant religious beliefs between 1538 and 1558. Among those known to have undergone this horrific death was Robert Samuel, a minister from East Bergholt in 1555, Alexander Gooch of Woodbridge and Alice Driver of Grundisburgh, both burnt on the same day in the town in 1558, and Agnes Potten and Joan Trunchfield who were burned together in 1556.

THE BURY WITCH TRIAL

At the height of his notoriety, 'The Witchfinder General' Matthew Hopkins was in great demand from the larger market towns of Eastern England to bring along his team and search for witches. Contemporary records state that almost 200 persons had been detained as suspected witches for the 1645 Sessions at Bury St Edmunds. In the 'True relation of the Arraignment of Witches That were Tried, Convicted and Condemned at Sessions at St Edmunds-bury' the following eighteen names are listed as those who had been tried, found guily and executed by hanging for witchcraft, at Bury on 27 August 1645:

John Lowes (80-year-old rector of Brandeston)
Thomas and Mary Everard (husband and wife)
Mary Bacon
Anne Alderman
Rebecca Morri
Mary Fuller
Mary Clowes
Margery Sparham
Katherine Tooley

Sarah Spinlow
Jane Limstead
Anne Wright
Mary Smith
Jane Rivers
Susan Manners
Mary Skipper
Anne Leech

MURDEROUS ATTACK
IN BURY CHURCHYARD

Edwin Crisp had been enjoying the New Year festivities for 1721 at the home of his brother-in-law Arundel Coke, when Coke suggested that they should step out for a while and visit Mrs Monk's coffee house. As the pair walked through the Bury churchyard, Crisp was attacked by John Woodburn wielding a billhook. Coke returned to his home, stating that he had decided to walk home alone – truth was he was not expecting to see Edwin alive again. But – lo! – a hideous vision walked into the festivities; throat cut, both cheeks cut and nose split in two, horribly injured but very much alive, it was Edwin Crisp! The news of the terrible deed soon spread across the town but it remained unsolved until local blacksmith John Carter, fearing he would be dragged into the affair, told the authorities he had been approached by Coke to assassinate Crisp. It transpired Coke's sister stood to inherit Crisp's money if he died (his children all having died previously – possibly poisoned by Coke). After temporary loss of speech, Crisp recovered his voice and revealed what he knew and Coke and Woodburn were soon on trial. Both found guilty, they were executed on 31 March 1721. Coke paid for a quiet execution at 6 a.m., while Woodburn went to his death in front of a huge crowd on Tayfen Meadows.

THE PRODIGAL SON

One of the most notorious cases of murder to rock the county of Suffolk in the eighteenth century was that of the rich and spoilt Charles Drew Jnr. As his money ran low he borrowed from friends and became involved in smuggling, and his father was quite fed up with his son's irresponsible behaviour. The final straw came when he heard the boy had got the housekeeper of Liston Hall pregnant and he cut off his allowance. Fatally, however, he did not cut the boy out of his will. Failing to find an assassin to do the dirty work for him, the prodigal son borrowed a gun and shot his father on the doorstep of his home on Hall Street, Long Melford. Humphries, a confederate of young Drew, was accused of the murder and sent to Bury Gaol. A letter was smuggled out to Drew, pleading for help, but was delivered in error to Timothy Drew. The game was up and constables were soon detailed to trace Charles Jnr. He was arrested in London, detained at Newgate and brought in irons with a heavy escort to Bury to stand trial in March 1740. Humphries saved his skin by turning King's Evidence and ensured Drew kept his appointment with the hangman.

SMUGGLERS

Suffolk has a long history of smuggling. 'Giffling' Jack Corbolt was a respectable innkeeper by day and violent smuggler by night. In July 1745, Giffling Jack and his team of fifty smugglers ran a massive cargo of tea and brandy ashore at Benacre Warren. Customs authorities estimated that by this time 4,500 horse-loads of contraband had been run across the Suffolk beaches since the year had begun and action had to be taken. After dogged pursuits and many abortive traps, the excisemen eventually captured Giffling Jack and some of his cronies. Held in a secure cell, Giffling Jack was transported to Norwich for trial. A team of experienced riding officers were charged with this duty but were outnumbered and outgunned by a twenty-man ambush and Giffling Jack escaped into the night again.

THE HADLEIGH GANG

One of the most infamous and outstandingly successful bands of smugglers was the Hadleigh Gang, who ran hundreds of wagon-loads of contraband goods, especially brandy and tea, into hideouts around the Suffolk countryside. On the night of 30 May 1746, about eighty of their number gathered at Cheverton, armed to the teeth with pistols, cutlasses, clubs and daggers. They ran about 50 hundredweight of 'tea from parts beyond the sea from which goods customs due to His Majesty'. The only man to be apprehended after this incident was arrested after a reward of some £500 was offered for any of the gang's capture. He happened to be one of the gang leaders, a John Harvey of Pond Hall near Hadleigh. Witnesses attested to seeing Harvey, armed with his brace of pistols, helping run the goods ashore and take his share at the end. Found guilty, Harvey was sentenced to seven years' transportation.

HE WHO BETRAYS THE SMUGGLERS

Smugglers sought out the Beccles home of Henry Hurrell in March 1745, having received information that he was an informant. Breaking in through a window, they rushed in and dragged him from his bed. Outside, they stripped the bleary eyed man, whipped him mercilessly, tied his semi-conscious body to a horse, and then rode off with him. Although a reward of £50 was offered for news of his fate, nothing was ever seen of him again.

TOLD IN STONE

A gravestone in Bungay Holy Trinity Church is inscribed: 'To the memory of Henry Scarles who was valued when alive, and respected now dead, was cruelly murdered at Whitacre, Burgh on 10th of February 1787 in the 23rd year of his age.' According to contemporary accounts, Scarle was a servant of Mattias Kerrison, a merchant at the staithe at Bungay. On that fateful night, William Hawke of Beccles and Thomas Mayhew of Bungay, with accomplice Simon Stannard, set about robbing one of Kerrison's corn lighters and were disturbed by Scarle. Fired up by the situation the robbers set about beating Scarles, pushed him into the water and struck him on the head with a quant while he was struggling. Laying low in the locality for a short time, they were apprehended at Botesdale by 'persons employed by the Bungay Association'. Taken to Norwich Castle, Stannard turned King's Evidence and saw Hawke and Mayhew stand trial and be found guilty. They were hanged on Norwich Castle Hill the following March.

EARLY NINETEENTH-CENTURY GAOLS AND BRIDEWELLS IN SUFFOLK

County Gaol, Ipswich
Beccles Bridewell
Bury Bridewell
  (now Moyse's Hall Museum)
Bury St Edmunds Gaol
Clare Bridewell

Ipswich Borough Gaol
Ipswich Bridewell
Lavenham Bridewell
Mildenhall Bridewell
Sudbury Gaol and Bridewell
Woodbridge Bridewell

LAST WITCH AND WIZARD TO BE SWUM
FOR WITCHCRAFT IN SUFFOLK

In the course of examining a pauper at the Angel Inn, Stanningfield, in June 1792, Justices Sir Charles Danvers and Revd John Ord were shocked to hear her accuse another old lady of being a witch and of having 'disordered her head'. The justices explained they could take no cognisance of the accusation but notwithstanding the accused lady submitted to the usual ordeal the following Wednesday. At first it was proposed to weigh her against the church bible, but the local rector refused to lend it for the purpose. Undaunted, the woman's husband, brother and another man tied a rope around her body and cast her into a horse pond. She promptly sank and had to be pulled out in an almost lifeless state. The men, especially her husband, were rebuked for putting the woman through this ordeal but he argued he thought it better to 'indulge her therein, than to suffer her destroy herself, which was certain she would have done had she not undergone the trial'.

The last man to be swum, in order to discover if he was a wizard, was 67-year-old Isaac Stebbings, in the Grimmer Pond at Wickham Skeith in 1825. He had been accused of overlooking his neighbours

with the evil eye. Combined with a few other strange coincidences or concoctions of imagination, Stebbings wanted to clear the air of these accusations and offered to be swum. After being escorted by villagers and many from the surrounding settlements to the pond, four men lifted him onto his back and there he floated on the surface for ten minutes – much to the frustration of the crowd. Someone shouted 'Give him another', and the process was repeated. The crowd wanted a dunking and shouted, 'Try him again and dip him under'. One of the men in the water put his foot on Stebbings' chest only to have Stebbings' feet come up as he went under. This trial saw poor old Stebbings in the water for almost an hour and resulted in him being totally exhausted. The crowd were still not satisfied and wanted another test carried out the following week, but the local clergy and churchwardens would have no more of this abomination, and the following week when the crowds drew up they were sent away by the clerics!

GAOL BREAK!

George Mann escaped from Woodbridge Gaol in 1836 by detaching an iron spike which had formed one of the bars of his cell. He set about removing bricks from the bottom of his cell wall in an area not visible to any warder in the prison. Working hard from between the hours of about ten or eleven in the morning until three in the afternoon, he removed about 100 bricks. Mann then dropped through the hole, down the 12 or 13ft into the prison garden and was off. However, he was soon missed, and a search was mounted. He was found at Witnesham at about six the same evening. The prison report on the incident concluded: 'No blame could be attached to anyone in this matter as the walls of the prison were severely unsound.'

THE DUAL PURPOSE CRANE

In 1477 a crane was erected on the common quay in Ipswich. This device had a secondary purpose to the loading and unloading of cargo; scolds could be suspended from it over the Orwell, and if they really did need cooling down, they could be strapped into the ducking stool and dunked in the waters.

PILLORIED

Ipswich pillory was erected in Cornhill and used as punishment for a variety of misdemeanours such as drunkenness, perjury and salacious speech, and also stood as a warning and punishment for dishonest tradesmen who would fiddle their weights and measures, and pollute or dilute their goods to make them go further. In the eighteenth century, the courts would hand down the penalty of a two-hour stand for a first offence; for a second it was eight hours of abuse, with rotten fruit, dead animals and excrement being hurled at you.

MAXIMUM LOAD FOUR PERSONS

The largest number of convicted felons to be dropped at the same time on the gallows in Suffolk was four. The men hanged were despatched before a massive crowd at Bury St Edmunds on 21 April 1824. They were:

    John Chenery (aged 23) of Beccles
    Benjamin Howlett (aged 23) of Exning
    Thomas Wright (aged 26) of Gelmsford
    Robert Bradman (aged 28) of Glemsford

All of them were hanged for burglary.

LAST MAN HANGING

The last man to be executed at Bury St Edmunds was 23-year-old George Cant, who was hanged for the murder of Mary Payne on 22 April 1851.

MURDER AT THE RECTORY

On the morning of Sunday, 8 May 1853 the aged Revd Barker took his young servant girl to church and left Mrs Maria Steggles, his equally aged housekeeper (they were both in their eighties), to cook the lunch. On their return from church they entered the kitchen to discover a scene akin to a slaughterhouse. Mrs Steggles was on the floor and blood from the wounds inflicted on her head and gash to her throat spattered across the walls, across her open prayer book and smashed glasses. Suspicion immediately fell on 18-year-old William Flack, who had recently been dismissed from the reverend's employment. Flack was known to bear a grudge against Mrs Steggles and had been was heard to say he would soon 'steal some of the old parson's mouldy sovereigns'. His mouth did not endear him to the assizes either, as he tried to implicate another in the crime, but when convicted he openly confessed he had rung the bells for Sunday service and, having 'chimed the parson in', ran to the rectory and committed the murder. William Flack was executed at Ipswich Gaol on 16 August 1853.

BUNGAY WATCH

When the Bungay Watch (a localised forerunner of the police force) was created in 1819 the terms of its appointment stipulated that between 20 February and 1 May a watch was to be maintained every night from the hours of ten until five o'clock in the morning, and the parish constable was to superintend them. Watchmen were to be paid 14s a week. Lanthorns and alarm rattles were supplied by the council but both constable and the watchmen had to supply their own candles!

THE RED BARN MURDER

The crime that became known as the 'Red Barn Murder' is the most infamous crime committed in Suffolk; indeed, it drew such national interest that it became one of the most infamous of the entire nineteenth

century. William Corder was the son of a prosperous farmer of Polstead in Suffolk. In 1826, he began a relationship with Maria Marten, who was no shrinking violet, having had more than one lover and borne at least one illegitimate child before she had the relationship with Corder. In 1827 she gave birth at the rooms she shared with Corder at Sudbury. This male child apparently died soon after Maria's return to Polstead and was buried (and remains undiscovered) somewhere in the village. On 18 May 1827, Corder told Maria to make discreet preparations to travel to Ipswich where they would be married. She was to meet him in the evening at the Red Barn disguised as a man and they would make their elopement.

Maria made her way to the barn and was never seen alive again. Corder reappeared at Polstead a few days later, stating that he had left Maria at Ipswich, before he departed for London where he began advertising for a wife. He soon set up a school with Mary Moore, his new bride, in Brentford. Maria's mother dreamt her daughter was dead and buried under the dirt floor of the Red Barn. Persuading her mole-catcher husband to investigate, old Mr Marten found his wife's dream proved to be horribly true and the body of Maria was unearthed on 19 April 1828 – she had been shot and apparently stabbed. Corder was brought back to Polstead for trial but he claimed she had shot herself and vehemently denied stabbing her. The witnesses and evidence, however, piled up against him and he was found guilty and sentenced to death.

The governor of Bury St Edmunds Gaol, John Orridge, implored Corder to confess, to which he acceded with the words 'I am a guilty man' and produced a written confession that he signed on the morning of his execution on 11 August 1828. But Corder always maintained he did not stab Maria – perhaps her father's small mole spade, driven into the ground while searching for her, caused her wounds. The trial and execution of Corder drew great interest in the local and national press; over a million broadsides were claimed to have been sold and even ceramic figurines and models of the Red Barn were produced as souvenirs, and a number of books and plays have been written about the crime.

THE GREAT COACH ROBBERY

The London to Ipswich mail coach was carrying a clerk from Alexander & Co. whose task was to deliver £30,000 worth of the bank's own £10, £5 and £1 notes to its Ipswich office. The clerk claimed he watched the box at all times, keeping it beside him while travelling, and on the two refreshment stops left the coach door open so he could observe the box at all times. When the coach arrived at Ipswich the box had been tampered with and when opened was empty! Alexander & Co. printed a new batch of notes in red and put announcements in the press that none of their previous notes, which were printed in black, should be accepted. The crime remains an unsolved enigma.

THE RECTOR OF WETHERINGSETT

George Wilfred Frederick Ellis, aged 35, was appointed curate at Wetheringsett in 1883. He proved to be a popular priest with the locals as he performed baptisms, marriages, funerals and regular services in the village until, by chance, he was found out and exposed as a fraud impersonating a priest. Ellis's paperwork proved to be forged and he was apprehended by Inspector Bly of Eye in March 1888. In a trial where the Lord Bishop of Norwich gave evidence, the jury were left in no doubt of the answers given on oath and returned a verdict of 'Guilty' without leaving their box. Ellis was sentenced to seven years penal servitude in Dartmoor Prison. The matter did, however, leave a legacy behind in the village. Where did the people stand who had been married by Ellis over the five years of his tenure? Were they still married or not, and did this make their children bastards? A special Act of Parliament had to be drawn up recognising all of Ellis' marriages 'as valid as if the same had been solemnised before a duly ordained clergyman of the Church of England'.

THE PEASENHALL HORROR

Second only in notoriety to the Red Barn Murder is the Murder of Rose Annie Harsent at Providence House, Peasenhall, on 1 June 1902. Rose Harsent, aged 23, was a local girl employed at Providence House, the home of Mr and Mrs William Crisp. Her father, William Harsent, came round at 8 a.m. to bring her clean washing. Finding the back entrance open, he stepped inside to discover his daughter lying dead in a pool of blood on the floor. Upstanding local man William Gardiner was the prime suspect. He was married, but local boys had put about a rumour that he and Rose had been heard behaving inappropriately together while alone in a local chapel. The gossipmongers got to work and in November William Gardener was on trial at Ipswich for the murder.

The presented evidence did not convince all the jurors and they could not agree – eleven for conviction, one for acquittal. Tried again the following January the same thing happened – eleven for, one against. The case was declared *nolle prosequi* – in effect, the law gave up and Gardiner was released on 29 January 1903. Gardiner felt he could not return to Peasenhall; his name had not been cleared so he shaved his beard off and disappeared into obscurity in London.

POLICE FORCE DISMISSED!

The Ipswich Borough Police was brought into existence on 1 March 1836 but went into sharp decline after just over six years of good work, following the loss of two good superintendents. Disciplinary offences became rife; the police barrack block was situated near St Mary le Tower Church and complaints of disorderly conduct came thick and fast on Sundays from members of the church congregation who observed law officers drinking and 'using improper language'. Women staying in the single men's quarters were also noted! The force was described as being in 'a deplorable state of affairs' so the Ipswich Watch Committee undertook drastic measures and dismissed the entire establishment on 5 August 1842.

THE BURNING OF THE BATH HOTEL

Acting as part of a national arson campaign to force action in favour of the Votes for Women cause, suffragettes Evaline Hilda Birkitt and Florence Olivia Tunks burned down the Bath Hotel at Felixstowe on 29 May 1914. Always attempting to ensure the safety of others but maximise their militant actions, the women knew the Bath Hotel was empty for refurbishment in anticipation of the summer season. The hotel 'went up like a torch' and little could be done to save it. Luggage tickets bearing suffragette campaign statements were discovered by a police officer at the scene. Birkitt and Tunks were soon identified as strangers to the town and were arrested after refusing to give their names or reveal their addresses. These suffragette arsonists were sent for trial and caused uproar in court. Both were found guilty – Birkitt was sentenced to two years and Tunks nine months. True to their cause they didn't go quietly and even went on hunger strike while in Holloway. After the First World War these outrageous acts were all but forgotten and these Suffragette heroines faded into obscurity and lived to ripe old ages.

RIOT!

The Ancient Order of Forresters Annual Gala at Walsham-le-Willows of July 1911 was in full swing when an argument broke out about the change given on the Steam Horses at the travelling fair. Matters got out of hand quickly and a group of local men set about trying to wreck the Steam Horses, while some of the fair folk shot at them with rifles from the target stall. Serious shooting broke out when locals fetched their shotguns from their homes. Seven men had received bullet wounds by the time the landlord of the Anchor at Blo'Norton public house just happened to be passing the field in his pony and trap. A stray shot fatally wounded the man, and it was only after this tragic act that order and peace began to descend on Walsham again.

FIRST UNIFORMED POLICEWOMAN

The first uniformed Ipswich Police Matron was recruited in May 1924. The position was filled by 26-year-old Miss Adelaide Bryant, her primary responsibility being to attend to women in custody.

ADMINISTERING THE LAW

During the eighteenth and nineteenth centuries, Suffolk judges were included in the Norfolk Circuit of Judges, and the assizes were held at Ipswich and Bury St Edmunds alternately (usually Spring Assizes at Bury, Summer Assizes at Ipswich). Quarter Sessions for the different divisions of the county were held at Ipswich, Bury St Edmunds, Beccles and Woodbridge. The County Gaol for Suffolk was erected on St Helen's Street, Ipswich, in 1790. The old county courts were erected in front of the County Gaol 1836–37.

THE WORTHAM TITHE WAR

Eighteen days in February 1934 saw one of the most bizarre actions in Suffolk during the twentieth century. In what should have been a localised incident, Mr Rash, a Wortham gentleman farmer, had refused to pay his tithes under protest and the county bailiffs moved in to seize and impound 134 pigs and 15 bullocks from his farm. Hearing of his plight and in search of a cause, about fifty of Sir Oswald Moseley's Blackshirts descended on the farm, hoisted their black flag beside the union flag and made plans to thwart the removal of the livestock by fortifying the farm with barbed wire, obstacles and mounting patrols. These actions were unprecedented and drew national newspaper coverage, and thousands came to watch from all over the country. About 100 police officers were drafted into the village in two buses, not only to check the Blackshirts but to deal with the congestion caused by the vehicles of the spectators on the country roads.

Eventually the police were given the authority to break the deadlock and advanced to make arrests. The Blackshirts immediately took up defensive positions and issued taunts but the arrests were made peacefully, much to the bewilderment of the onlookers. At dawn on 22 February a convoy of lorries, county bailiffs and police arrived at the farm, equipped to tackle all of the fortifications. The police linked arms to restrain the crowd, clods of earth were thrown and a few helmets knocked off but within two hours the cattle were removed and the Wortham Tithe War was over. Tithes were abolished in 1936 and all that remains today is a squat pillar at the junction of lanes above the church bearing the enigmatic legend: 'The Tithe War. 134 pigs and 15 cattle (value £702) seized for tithe February 22nd 1934.'

8

TRANSPORT

LAST OF THE SEDAN CHAIR CLERICS

The Reverend Alfred William Snape, vicar of St Mary's Church, Bury St Edmunds, is believed to have been the last rector to make regular use of a sedan chair as a means of conveyance to and from church. He preached his last sermon shortly before his death, aged 70, in 1896.

SCARESHIPS

In May 1909, newspapers were full of accounts of an unexplained luminous airship seen traversing the country from as far apart as Wales and Suffolk. (To put this event into perspective, the Wright brothers only achieved powered flight in 1903, Bleriot would not fly across the Channel until two months later and the first channel crossings by airship were a year away.) Panic occurred in certain quarters; talk of these mysterious Zeppelins led to suggestions that their purpose was sinister. One persistent idea was that these airships were spying for Germany. Mr J.W. Stockman, the skipper of a Lowestoft trawler, stated that when he saw the airship he was some 35 miles from Lowestoft. The third hand called him on deck and he discerned what at first seemed to be a star rising then saw a cigar-shaped form in the sky, similar to the pictures of airships the skipper had seen; he was confident it was not a balloon. Stockman burned a red flare which was answered by a red flare from the airship overhead. He then burnt a white flare and the airship answered with a blue one. The skipper concluded that if the airship carried on its tack observed over the trawler, 'it would have ended up to the North of Holland and over Holland to Germany'.

LAST WORDS ON THE WAGGONER

Palgrave Waggoner John Catchpole died on 16 July 1787 aged 87. His epitaph reads:

> My horses have done running,
> My Waggon is decay'd,
> And now in the Duft my Body is lay'd
> My whip is worn & my work
> It is done
> And now I'm brought here to my laft home.

FLORY'S OMNIBUS

DURING THE SUMMER MONTHS,

To the "Bath Hotel," FELIXSTOW,

Leaving the " COACH & HORSES " Inn, IPSWICH, EVERY MORNING at NINE, returning at SIX p.m.

MILESTONES

The cast-iron milestones on what is now the A12 between Ipswich and Lowestoft were made in Ipswich at the ironworks of Jacob Garrett (1774–1833).

Jacob's brother Richard (1755–1839) founded Garrett's Engineering Works at Leiston where 'The Long Shop', one of the earliest flow-line production assembly halls in the world, was built 1852–53.

Richard Garrett's Engineering Works of Leiston made their first undertype steam wagon in 1904. It was developed so successfully that the 'Garrett' was recognised as one of the finest wagons of this type on the road in its day.

PADDLE STEAMER TO...

In the 1930s there were regular paddle steamers services from Felixstowe aboard such vessels as the *City of Rochester* – the fares in 1933 were:

Afternoon Sea Cruises

Adults	2s
Children under 14 years	1s
Day Return to Clacton	2s
Day Return to Walton	1s 9d
Single to Southend	4s 6d
Single to Gravesend	4s
Single to London	4s
Single to Harwich	9d
Single to Ipswich	1s

LAST TRAIN DEPARTED

(Redundant or lost railway stations in Suffolk, noting which company built them and the years they were open)

Aldeburgh, East Suffolk Railway, 1860–1966
Bentley, Eastern Union Railway, 1946–1966
Bungay, Waveney Valley Railway, 1860–1964
Claydon, Ipswich, Bury and Norwich Railway, 1846–1963
Corton, Norfolk and Suffolk Joint Railway, 1903–1970
Eye, Mellis and Eye Railway, 1867–1931
Felixstowe Beach, Felixstowe Railway and Pier Company, 1877–1967

Framlingham, East Suffolk Railway, 1859–1952
Hacheston Halt, Great Eastern Railway, 1922–1952
Hadleigh, Eastern Union & Hadleigh Junction Railway, 1847–1965
Haverhill, Great Eastern Railway, 1865–1967
Ipswich Stoke Hill, Eastern Union Railway, 1846–1860
Lowestoft North, Norfolk and Suffolk Joint Railway, 1903–1970
Marlesford, Great Eastern Railway, 1859–1952
Mildenhall, Great Eastern Railway, 1885–1962
Southwold, Southwold Railway Company, 1879–1929
Thorpeness, Great Eastern Railway, 1914–1966
Walberswick, Southwold Railway, 1879–1929
Yaxley Halt, Great Eastern Railway, 1922–1931

FLYING BOATS OVER FELIXSTOWE

Felixstowe Air Station opened on 5 August 1913 under the command of the wonderfully named Wing Commander C.E. Risk.

By the end of the First World War, RAF Felixstowe was the biggest coastal air station in the world.

Famous officers who served at Felixstowe include Flying Officer Frank Whittle, the inventor of the jet engine, and a certain Aircraftman 1st Class T.E. Shaw – real name Colonel T.E. Lawrence CB, DSO (also known as 'Lawrence of Arabia') – the famed author, poet and distinguished Army officer renowned for his role during the Sinai and Palestine Campaigns and the Arab Revolt during the First World War.

When the Felixstowe Fury flying boat, with its wingspan of 123ft, was introduced in 1918 it had the largest wingspan of any aircraft in the world.

On 12 August 1924, the King's Cup air race had its start at Felixstowe.

Aircraft from RAF Felixstowe regularly competed for the Schneider Trophy and were often well placed. They won it in 1927 when the competition was hosted in Venice, Italy, when Flight Lieutenant Sidney Webster flew his Supermarine S.5 N.220 at an average speed of 281.65mph.

The first WAAF's to be stationed at RAF Felixstowe arrived in 1949.

RAF Felixstowe had its last inspection by an Air Officer in April 1961, No.33 Wing RAF left in March 1962 and it finally closed as an RAF base on 21 June 1962.

LONDON TO MELBOURNE AIR RACE … IN MILDENHALL?

The one-off London to Melbourne Air Race for the MacRobertson Trophy (staged as part of the Melbourne Centenary celebrations) actually had its competitors take off from Mildenhall at 6.30 a.m. on 20 October 1934. The race drew massive interest; thousands of spectators descended upon the aerodome, and the Prince of Wales was the guest of honour. The race saw the aircraft travel approximately 11,300 miles via five compulsory stops at Rome, Allahabad, Singapore, Darwin and Charleville. A further twenty-two optional stops were also provided with stocks of fuel at such exotic locations as Athens, Baghdad, Rangoon, Bangkok and Singapore.

The finish line of the race was Flemington racecourse, Melbourne, flown over by outright winners British pilots Charles William Anderson 'C.W.A.' Scott and Tom Campbell Black in the de Haviland 88 Comet 'Grosvenor House' (G-ACSS), who completed the flight that had been estimated to have required eighty-six hours in just seventy-six hours and eighteen seconds.

IPSWICH AIRPORT

The 147-acre Ravens Wood site was purchased by the Ipswich Corporation in 1929 with the intention of creating a municipal airport. Work proceeded apace and Ipswich Airport was officially opened by Prince Edward (later King Edward VIII) on 26 June 1930. Described when it was opened as 'one of the finest in the county', its terminal building, designed by Hening and Chitty, is a Grade II listed building. Sadly, times were not good for the airport in the 1990s and after a development report was commissioned for the site, the findings stated that the site could be better used for development. The airfield closed in 1993 and was finally de-licensed and ceased to be registered by the Civil Air Authority in 1996. The site has now been redeveloped as the Ravenswood housing estate.

9

FOOD
AND DRINK

SOME TRADITIONAL TASTES OF SUFFOLK

Suffolk Rusks
Rub ¼lb butter into ½lb flour; add a pinch of salt and a pinch of baking
powder. Mix into a stiff paste with an egg and very little milk. Roll out,
cut into rounds and bake in a hot oven until risen (about ten minutes).
Then take out, pull in half and put back rough side up to brown. Best
eaten on the day of baking!

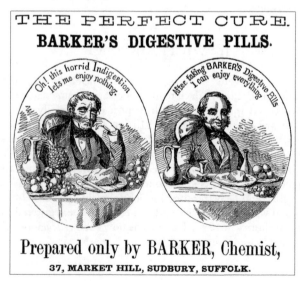

THE PERFECT CURE.
BARKER'S DIGESTIVE PILLS.

Oh! this horrid Indigestion lets me enjoy nothing.

After taking BARKER'S Digestive Pills I can enjoy everything

Prepared only by BARKER, Chemist,
37, MARKET HILL, SUDBURY, SUFFOLK.

Southwold Bacon and Onion Dumpling

Make a suet crust with ½lb of flour, ¼lb suet and about a gill of water. Roll out flat to oblong shapes, about 9x14in. Spread evenly with rashers of bacon and chopped onion. Season with salt, pepper and chopped sage. Roll up, tie in a pudding cloth and steam for three hours. Excellent with spinach or broccoli.

Shrimp Pie

Pick a quart of brown shrimps, place in a greased pie dish, and season with mace, clover and anchovy essence. Pour over them 1tbspn of melted butter and one glass of sharp white wine. Cover with thin short crust pastry, glaze with egg and bake in a hot oven.

Neave's Recipe for Suffolk Glazed Ham

Mix together 1dstspn of runny honey, 2dstspns of soft sugar, 1dstspn of dry or made mustard, and few drops of water to form a stiff paste. Score the fat of the ham into a diamond pattern. Spread the mixture over the ham and heat for five to ten minutes in a hot oven until caramelised. Decorate with cherries or slices of fruit if wished, then fold the ham frill in half lengthways, wind round knuckle bone and pin underneath.

Traditional Suffolk Ham

Take fresh leg of pork and brine it using a solution containing saltpetre. Pickle the brined leg for three weeks or more in a mix of blacktreacle, sugar, salt and either stout, strong ale, cider or port wine and add a mix of spices to taste. Remove from the pickle mix then smoke the leg for four to five days over oak sawdust. The leg is then to be hung for at least a month before it is ready to eat.

Fourses Cake

(The afternoon snack for the agricultural working man)
Rub ½lb of lard into 2lb of flour. Add ½lb of sugar, ½lb currants and a good pinch of spices. Cream 1oz of yeast with a little sugar, mix with a pint of fresh milk. Stir in the flour mix and stand in a warm place to rise for an hour, then bake for one and a half hours in a hot oven.

Treacle Tart

Line a deep plate with shortcrust pastry. Beat an egg well, add 2tbspns of treacle. Pour into the pastry, grate with nutmeg, bake in a slow oven for forty minutes. Serve cold.

Mrs Goodman's Harvest Beer (Recorded in 1883)
Boil ½ pint of hops in 1 gallon of water for two hours. Strain and sweeten. Pour into an earthenware vessel then float a slice of toast on top with a spoonful of brewer's yeast on it. Cover and leave all night. Next day, remove toast, and skim the top, ready to serve. (This beer did not keep well and fresh supplies had to be made daily.)

SCHOOL DINNERS

The first organised canteen for an elementary school was started in the village school of Wangford – with Henham – in 1918, by the then headmaster Mr Ernest F. Easto and his wife, Alice. An early menu for the week records the meals as:

Monday: Suet pudding and gravy, mashed potatoes and carrots – Ginger baked squares and custard.
Tuesday: Meat and vegetable soup with bread – Jam tart.
Wednesday: Meat and vegetable pie with crust – Suet pudding with jam or treacle.
Thursday: Shepherd's pie with gravy – Currant pudding with custard.
Friday: Meat patties, potatoes, greens and gravy – Treacle or jam roll.

TASTY SUFFOLK TREATS OF TODAY

Fish and chips on the beach at Southwold or Aldeburgh
Butterworth & Son's Suffolk Regiment Malabar Chutney
A crusty loaf of bread from Pump Street Bakery in Orford
Newmarket sausages from Musks or Powters
Smoked fish pâté from Pinney's of Orford
Gressingham Duck
Red Poll beefburger produced by Allan's Farm, Ubbeston
Broxtead Banger sausages
Alde Valley leg of lamb
A Blythburgh free range pork pie from Lawson's Deli, Aldeburgh
Sutton Hoo free range chicken
Calver's pure Suffolk honey
Suffolk cure ham from Neaves of Debenham
Hams and smoked meats from Emmett's or Creasey's of Peasenhall
Smoked cheese from the Artisan Smokehouse

Fresh, locally caught seafood at the Butt and Oyster at Pin Mill
A meal at the Leaping Hare at Wyken Vineyard
Suffolk Mud Bloody Mary Ketchup
Brunch at Twyfords Café, Beccles
Alder Carr fruit ice cream
Chocolate brownie from the Wild Strawberry Café, Woodbridge
A bar of Deepmills Dark Chocolate with Ginger
A tasty tart from Leo's deli at Framlingham
A cafetiere of Paddy and Scott's Great with Friends coffee
Squirrell (yes, no joke) from the Wild Meat Company of Blaxhall

AND TO DRINK

Maynard House Orchards Apple Juice
Aspall's Cyder
Wissett Wines' Noah's Flood dry white wine
Venus red wine from Shawsgate Vineyard
Calvors Lager of Coddenham Green

Suffolk folk

insist on

TOLLY

for

QUALITY

A SELECTION OF SUFFOLK BEERS

Broadside 4.7%, Adnams, Southwold
Gisleham Gold 4.5%, Trinity Ales, Gisleham
Rattlesden Best Bitter 4%, Cox & Holbrook, Buxhall
Bungay Dark Mild 3.4%, Green Dragon, Bungay
Trawlerboys 4.6%, Green Jack, Lowestoft
Black Shuck 4.2%, Hellhound Brewing Ltd, Hadleigh
Bildeston Porter 4.6%, King's Head Brewing Co., Bildeston
Strong Suffolk 6%, Greene King, Bury St Edmunds
The Suffolk 5%, Harwich Town Brewing Co., Harwich
Tornado Smith 4.3%, Mill Green Brewery, Edwardstone
St. Edmund's Head 5%, Old Cannon Brewery, Bury St Edmunds
Suffolk Gold 4.9%, St Peter's Brewery, South Elmham
Cherry Stout 4.8%, Bartram's, Rougham
Ufford Tipple 3.7%, Uffa Brewery, Woodbridge
Suffolk Pride 4.1%, Cliff Quay, Debenham
Suffolk n See 4.6%, Tindall, Seething
Black Adder 5.3%, Mauldon's, Sudbury
Harwich Charter Beer 10%, Elveden Ales, Elveden
Umbel Ale (Special Coriander Ale) 3.8%, Nethergate Brewery, Clare
Old Ipswich Liquor 5.5%, Dove Street Brewery, Ipswich
Victoria Bitter 3.6%, E.S.B. (Earl Soham Brewery) Earl Soham
Waxie's Dargle 4%, Brandon Brewery

BAD BEER

In 1832 a Mildenhall brewer was caught using vitriol, Guinea pepper, cocculus, opium, capsicum, gum arabic, steel filings and sulphate of iron with turmeric to brew his beer. The process he had adopted used gum arabic to make it frothy, the steel to make it clear and the sulphate of iron and turmeric to colour it. He professed by these means to be able to make one quarter of malt do for three!

SOME SUFFOLK VARIETIES OF APPLE

Beauty of Livermere
Bradbury
Catherine – Grown for well over a century, this variety is only
    foundin the garden of the former Live and Let Live public house at
    Combs, near Stowmarket

Clopton Red – Raised by Justin Brooke of Wickhambrooke
   Nurseries in 1946

Emerline – Grown in Lowestoft

Honey Pippin – Developed by Justin Brooke of Wickhambrook
   Nurseries during the 1950s

Livermere Favourite – Raised by Mr Tallack of Bury St Edmunds

Lord Suffolk

Lady Henniker – Raised from a seedling in the 1840s at Thornham
   Hall, the home of the Henniker family at the time

Lord Stradbroke – Found or raised by Mr Fenn, Lord Stradbroke's
   head gardener at Henham Hall, near Wangford, in around 1900

Maclean's Favourite – Raised by Dr Allan Maclean of Sudbury, about 1820

Old Blake – Recorded as being grown in and around Blundeston
   since the late nineteenth century

Red Miller's Seedling – arose in the garden of Mr Wheldon of
   Sudbury in the 1940s

Ruby – Grown in and around Ipswich

St Edmunds's Pippin (also known as the St Edmund's Russet) –
   Raised by Mr Harvey of Bury St Edmunds, recorded as an
   established variety since the 1870s

Suffolk Beaufin

Suffolk Beauty

Suffolk Foundling

Suffolk Pink – Raised during the 1980s and '90s by Dan Neuteboom
   at his orchards at Braiseworth, from a strain first noticed at a
   nursery in Thurston in the 1970s

Suffolk Superb

OTHER SUFFOLK FRUITS INCLUDE...

Suffolk Thorn is a pear recorded as an established breed in the 1840s,
raised by Andrew Arcedeckne at Glevering Hall, Hacheston near
Wickham Market.

The greengage is so named after Thomas Gage of Hengrave Hall who
imported a shipment of the fruit from France and began cultivating it in
the house gardens during the eighteenth century.

Coe's Golden Drop is a cross between a greengage and a plum introduced
to the country by nurseryman Jervaise Coe at Bury St Edmunds in the
late eighteenth century.

The St Martin Plum, also known as Coe's Late Red, was also introduced by Jervaise Coe at Bury St Edmunds in around 1800.

SUFFOLK CHEESE

Suffolk Cheese is also known as 'bang', 'trip', 'thump' and 'wonmil' – the latter name referring directly to it being a 'flet' cheese, a term which means it was made from 'won' (one) single or skimmed cow's milk. Bloomfield wrote of it:

> And, like the oaken shelf whereon 'tis laid
> Mocks the weak efforts of the bending blade;
> Or in the hog's trough rests in perfect spite,
> Too big to swallow, too hard to bite.

Daniel Defoe remarked that Suffolk had the best butter, but the worst cheese, in England.

In 1673, John Ray recorded the Suffolk saying: 'Hunger will break through stone walls or anything except Suffolk cheese.'

In the *Magna Britannia* (1730) there was some mitigation offered for Suffolk cheese. It was described: 'Though not generally esteemed at home, [it] is by many in Germany, France and Spain. Its undeniable quality which makes it as useful as the best cheese of England is that it bears the sea better than any and is in general vogue among sailors, especially on long voyages.'

Universal Magazine (1759) added: '[...] it is much better for long voyages by reason of its dryness and the sea so mellows it that it has been sold for 12*d* per pound.'

But it was all in vain, as the *Ipswich Journal* of 16 June 1759 published the following notice:

> To Suffolk Farmers – the Suffolk Cheese being so badly made for some years past, the Lords of the Admiralty have thought it fit to exclude it from the Royal Navy for one year. It is hoped the dairymen will desist from making cheese from November till the beginning of May as it is of bad quality and has brought great odium to the country cheese.

In 1865, Walter White remarked that, 'Suffolk Cheese (at least, the sort given to labourers) is described as hard as grindstones, so hard that even rats and mice refuse it.'

There was even a little rhyme about Suffolk Cheese:

> Those that made me were uncivil,
> They made me harder than the Devil,
> Knives won't cut me; fire won't sweat me;
> Dogs bark at me, but can't eat me.

Sir Joshua Rowley of Tendring Hall attempted to revive Suffolk cheese making in 1900 but it did not take off. Only in more recent years has a more gourmet approach seen a new range of softer and very palatable Suffolk cheeses emerge, such as Buxlow Wonmil, Buxlow Paigle, Hawkston, Shipcord, Suffolk Gold and Suffolk Blue.

FUNERAL FARE

At Woodbridge the burial feast was called 'mulled-ale' and the dying person would have chosen what the bearers would have to drink. The bearers all had a drink before they went to church, while the mourners drank afterwards. All the mourners, even those not known for their religious observance, would not fail to attend church the following Sunday, when tradition held that the clergyman was obliged to preach a sermon from any text the mourners may choose.

10

MYTHS,
LEGENDS AND
CURIOSITIES

BLACK DOGS

Probably the most infamous of all
Suffolk tales is that of the 'Black Dog'
(or Dogs) who made visitation to church
congregations at Bungay and Blythburgh
on 4 August 1577. According to the
contemporary account of *A Strange and
Terrible Wunder*, wrought very late in the
parish church of Bungay, the town
was in the grip of a great storm of pouring
rain, thunder and lightning whereby the rumbles were thought to shake
the church itself. The already fearful congregation were plunged into
blind terror as:

> [a] black dog, or the divel in such likeness (was seen), running along
> the body of the church with such great swiftness, and incredible
> haste among people, in a visible form and shape, passed between
> two persons, as they were kneeling upon their knees, and occupied
> in prayer as it seemed, wrung the necks of them bothe at one
> instant clene backward … (that they) strangely dyed … Passing
> by an other man of the congregation in the church, gave him such
> a gripe on the back, that therewith all he was presently drawen
> togither and shrunk up, as it were a piece of lether scorched in a
> hot fire; or as the mouth of a purse or bag drawen together with
> a string. The man, albeit hee was in so strange a taking, dyed not,
> but as it is thought yet alive.

A 'Devil dog' also manifested at Blythburgh where with an almighty clap of thunder the steeple fell in and smashed the font, then 'the like thing entred, in the same shape and similitude' placed himself on a beam and swung into the church where he 'slew two men and a lad & burned the hand of another person that was there among the rest of the company, of whom divers were blasted. This mischief thus wrought, he flew with wonderful force to no little feare of the assembly out of the church in a hideous and hellish likenes.'

Although no marks of the Devil dog's visit remain in Bungay Church, he is remembered on the town coat-of-arms. At Blythburgh meanwhile, deep scorch marks are still visible on the church door; some say they are from lightning, while others still maintain they are the lasting scratch marks left by its most unwanted visitor.

THE GREEN CHILDREN OF WOOLPIT

Fifteenth-century chronicler William of Newburgh recorded this remarkable story related to the village of Woolpit (known in those times as Wolfpittes, after the ancient trenches near the settlement). Newburgh records how two children crawled out of these trenches one harvest time. The youngsters, a boy and a slightly older girl, were green in colour. They wore dresses of some unknown stuffs and spoke in an unfamiliar language. These children were caught and taken to the village. where for months after they would eat nothing but beans. Gradually they lost their green colour. but the little boy died. Before the boy died, however, he and the little girl did learn English and were able to say they belonged to the land of St Martin in an unknown country. Their country was a Christian land and had churches. There was no sun there, only a faint twilight; but beyond a broad river there lay a land of light. One day, they were watching their father's sheep when they heard a loud noise like the ringing of the bells of St Edmunds Monastery. All at once they found themselves in the trenches by the reapers at Woolpit. The girl survived and married a man from Lynn.

THE ORFORD MERMAN

In a story recorded by Abbot Ralph of Coggeshall in 1207, a strange merman appears to have once been known at Orford. Writing about events which happened about forty years before the account, one stormy night some fishermen caught a monster in their nets 'resembling a man in size and form; his body was covered in hair but his head quite bald except for a long shaggy beard'. Taken to the Governor of Orford Castle the merman was fed on raw flesh, which it 'pressed with its hands' before eating. The beast could not speak, not even when the soldiery of the castle tortured the poor thing by hanging it up by its feet. Brought to the church, it showed no concept of reverence or belief. He sought his bed at sunset and stayed there till sunrise. Allowed to go into the sea, the monster seemed at its happiest when diving round the three lines of nets kept in the water to prevent his escape. One day, the merman tired of this captive and solitary life in the castle, swam under the nets to freedom and was never seen again.

THE SCIAPOD

One of the most unusual creatures to be depicted on any church architecture is the Scipod carved into a bench end at St Mary's Church, Dennington. Said to be an inhabitant of the desert, it is depicted lying on its back, knees bent with its feet (that are as long and as wide as its body) in the air above, acting as a sun shade.

SPONTANEOUS HUMAN COMBUSTION?

The last of the Ipswich witches, one Grace Pett, met her end in 1744. Pett had allegedly laid a curse on a local farmer's sheep. Superstition held that redress against the witch could be obtained by fastening one of the poor sheep to the ground by burying its feet in the earth then setting fire to the rest of the beast. The following morning, Grace Pett's body was found lying on the floor near her hearth. She had been burnt to a cinder, but her hands and feet and the boarded floor, on which she lay, were not even scorched.

THE QUEEN'S HEART?

Queen Anne Boleyn, second wife of King Henry VIII, stayed many times with her aunt, Almata Calthorpe, Lady of the Manor of Erwarton. Local legend told of how Queen Anne made secret arrangements with her uncle, Sir Philip Parker, that after her execution on 19 May 1536 her heart should be taken and smuggled away to be entombed in secret at the Church of St Mary at Erwarton. Such a tale could be easily disregarded as a flight of fantasy had not a small leaden casket, formed in the shape of a heart and covered with lime and dust, been uncovered by stonemasons attending to a bulge in the south wall of Erwarton Church in 1836. Ordered to open it, only a little black dust was found inside. Soldered up again, it was placed on a coffin in the Cornwallis vault beneath the organ.

ST EDMUND

Local folklore tells of how King Edmund, having evaded capture by the rampaging Danes in AD 870, was revealed to a newlywed couple crossing Goldbrook Bridge at Hoxne by the reflection of his golden spurs glinting in the sun. His hiding place thus discovered, Edmund was captured by the Danes, secured to an oak tree and scourged with whips and finally put to death by a volley of arrows, after which they beheaded him. His head was immediately snatched up by a wolf and taken to a secret spot, where the wolf guarded it until it could be reunited with Edmund's body and given a Christian burial. When Edmund's kinsmen came for the body, the wolf was seen guarding the head between its forepaws. Moved a safe distance away to Sutton, the head was buried and a small wooden chapel was erected over the spot. At this tiny chapel miracles began to happen – sight was restored to the blind and speech restored to the dumb. The body was found to be incorruptible and the head had become miraculously reunited with the body!

Edmund's body was removed thirty-three years after his death to Boedericsworth. From this humble settlement and shrine grew one of the most important religious houses and towns of Suffolk – Bury St Edmunds. The oak upon which Edmund was executed was venerated for generations until it split and collapsed in August 1843. Revealed by this split was an old arrowhead thought to have been contemporary with the martyrdom of Edmund. This remarkable find was noted in the address of Sir Arthur Harvey to the members of the Archaeological Institute in 1854. Shortly after the collapse of the tree, a stone monument was erected on the site and may still be seen today. The split trunk and branches of the ancient oak were left near where they fell until it gradually rotted away or fell prey to souvenir hunters.

St Edmund is said to have put a curse on Goldbrook Bridge. On his capture he is believed to have uttered a dreadful curse on all newlyweds who might cross the bridge from that day forward. The belief of the curse is so strong that even today newly married couples avoid crossing the bridge on their wedding day.

PRINCES IN THE TOWER –
THE SUFFOLK TALE

Sir James Tyrell of Gipping Hall is alleged by Tudor historians to have been the man who arranged for the 12-year-old uncrowned Edward V and his 10-year-old brother to be suffocated with pillows under the orders of their uncle so that he could usurp the throne and be crowned Richard III in 1483. However, there is a tradition in the county that the order was for the princes simply to 'disappear' and that the princes were removed to Gipping Hall with their mother and thence into obscurity under new, more humble names and identities.

CROMWELL'S HEAD AT WOODBRIDGE

Charles II wreaked terrible revenge on those who committed treason against his father – even though the leading protagonists were already dead. The bodies of the regicides Cromwell, Ireton and Bradshaw were unceremoniously disinterred from their graves, drawn on a sledge to Tyburn, and hung until sun down before they were beheaded. Parboiled and covered in pitch, the disembodied heads were impaled on spikes at Westminister Hall on the anniversary of Charles I's funeral. There Cromwell's head remained until it was brought down in a gale and was picked up by a sentry. After passing through a number of hands for various amounts of money, it was passed onto museum proprietor Herr du Puy, who informed visitors in 1710 that he could command 60 guineas for it. After being exhibited in a number of curiosity shows the head was given by the niece of the last show proprietor to the family doctor, Dr Josiah Henry Wilkinson, for safekeeping. She eventually sold it to him and down this family line it was passed to Canon Horace Wilkinson of Woodbridge.

During the 1930s, while in the hands of Canon Wilkinson, the head, still on its iron spike and a fragment of wooden pole, was scientifically examined by Dr Karl Pearson and Dr G.M. Morant, as well as Mr A. Dickson-Wright, surgeons who noted the evidence of the eight axe blows used to remove Cromwell's head, his 'reddish hair' and even 'The historical wart which Cromwell insisted on his portrait painters putting in, and there in the proper place was the depression from which it had been chipped'. The nose had been flattened during the beheading, almost all the teeth were gone and the lips broken to fragments but all the tests and comparisons proved that this was indeed the head of Oliver Cromwell. Canon Wilkinson eventually saw to it that Cromwell's head was given a fitting final resting place when he presented it to Cromwell's his old edifice of learning, Sidney Sussex College at Cambridge.

ANOTHER HEAD

Simon Theobald, born in Sudbury about 1316, took Holy Orders and progressed well in the Church to become one of the chaplains of Pope Innocent VI, and was despatched on a mission to Edward III of England in 1356. Simon was made Chancellor of Salisbury, and the Pope made him the Bishop of London in 1362, before he further progressed to become Archbishop of Canterbury in 1375 and was styled Simon of Sudbury. Sudbury crowned Richard II at Westminster Abbey in 1377 and was made Lord Chancellor of England by the new king in 1380. However, it was a time of disquiet, many peasants blamed Sudbury directly for their woes and when they rose up in rebellion in 1381 they attacked his property and seized upon the man himself, dragged him to Tower Hill and beheaded him – eventually. It took eight blows to part his head from his body. His body was later buried in Canterbury Cathedral, but his head, initially impaled on London Bridge, was taken down and returned to Sudbury where it is still preserved as a relic at the Church of St Gregory.

THE BLAXHALL STONE

A circular sandstone boulder near Stone Farm at Blaxhall has become notorious as the 'Blaxhall Stone'. One story suggests that, because the soil surrounding the area is free from large lumps of rock, that the stone 'must have grown there'. Another tale goes further to claim the stone was about the size of a small loaf or 'two fists' when it was first ploughed up during the nineteenth century and thrown down by the old ploughman on the spot where it has remained ever since. When examined today it is considerably larger – about 1.52m across and 0.6m high (at least when I measured it) – and it is estimated to weigh around five tons. It is believed, by some, to still be growing!

THE DRUID'S STONE

St Mary's churchyard in Bungay has a strange lump of granite embedded in the ground that measures roughly 60cm by 30cm and stands roughly

76cm high. Known as the 'Druid's Stone', it has acquired all manner of strange tales over the years, among them a cautionary tale of how children dance backwards around the stone seven times the Devil will appear.

SHAKE – FOR OLD TIME'S SAKE

Philip Thicknesse (1719–1792), former Lieutenant Governor of Landguard Fort, left direction in his will that after his death his right hand be cut off and sent to his son, Lord Audley, 'in hopes that such a sight may remind him of his duty to God, after having so long abandoned the duty he owed to a father who once affectionately loved him'.

WAYSIDE GRAVES

Until the 1850s people who committed suicide could not be buried in consecrated ground but rather a separate, distant area in the north of the churchyard where the body would be laid face down facing west. Many believed the restless spirits of those who took their own lives would 'walk' to harass those they left behind so they would be buried away from the town or village at a four-way crossroads so the ghost would not know which path to take to return. To ensure the body and ghost stayed down it would be 'pinned' with an oaken stake through the heart (a practice prohibited by Act of Parliament in 1823). Crowds would gather around the local sexton as he performed this duty at the wayside grave – even children would risk the wrath of their parents by creeping along and looking through the legs of those assembled at the grim rite.

There are a number of well-attested instances of this being carried out in Suffolk. The *Ipswich Journal* of 4 October 1783 records the case of Ballingdon millwright Mr Hurwood who committed 'self-murder' by taking arsenic in a fit of discontent. He was 'buried at the cross-way, with a stake driven through his body, near the Pound on Ballingdon Hill'. In 1794, Thomas Adams, an inmate of the Shipmeadow workhouse, stabbed himself with a penknife in the body and neck. Dying immediately, the inquest returned a verdict of wilful murder and Adams was buried beside the highway with a stake driven through his heart. Another example can be found in Mr Danbrook of Yoxford who shot himself at his breakfast table and was 'interred in the highway' in

1801. Nearby was the grave of another man who hanged himself in Martin's barn near Willow Marsh Road. These graves caused this area to become known as Dead Men's Corner. The graves were maintained by the respective surveyors and roadmen of Yoxford for many years afterwards until a pile of sugar beet covered them during the Second World War and they finally eroded away.

One of the most famous wayside graves in Suffolk is at an old pathway crossroads near Kesgrave. John Dobbs hanged himself in a fit of despair in a nearby barn on the Kesgrave Hall estate. Buried and pinned by the wayside, his grave mound was the subject of many local tales. Over the years the tales got taller and more fanciful, to the extent that some of the younger bucks didn't believe there was anyone buried under there at all. One night after a Harvest Horkey at The Bell a few hardy boys, fortified with fine Suffolk ales, went to investigate. They dug down into the mound and soon found the bones of poor John Dobbs. Most took flight and ran off but one particularly hard lad reached into Dobb's jaw and took a tooth as a souvenir and wore it on his watch chain for years after.

SPORTS ROUNDUP

CAMPEN

The game of campen, camp ball, or camping, occasionally described as football (a very distant ancestor of the modern game), was an ancient sport enjoyed in the eastern counties, and most villages and towns would have had a camping land or pightle where it

was played. In Suffolk the strongholds of the game were along the sea coast, especially in the villages on the line of Hollesley Bay between the rivers Orwell and Alde. Campen would have been played between even-numbered sides of brawny young men of the village and there would be occasional contests between neighbouring villages too, such as this match advertised in the *Ipswich Journal* in October 1754:

> On Monday 21st of this instant, October, there will be a match made by the gentlemen in the county of Suffolk (for ten men on ech side) to camp in a large field, adjoining to Cranley Green, in Eye, for five shillings a man.

Campen was played with a 'camp ball' made from a pig's bladder filled with horse hair and peas; the object of the game was to get the ball through the opposing team's goal which would have been marked by two posts that had been driven into the ground about 2-3ft apart at a distance of 150-200 yards from each other before the start of the match. An early description of a match stated:

> The players propel a huge ball, not by throwing it up into the air, but by striking and rolling it along the ground and not by their hands but by their feet, a game, I say, abominable enough ... and rarely ending but with some loss, accident, or disadvantage of the players themselves.

Indeed, it was rare for no breakages and cuts not to occur during a match. In *The Anatomy of Abuses in the Realm of England* (1583), the author classed football as a 'devilish pastime ... more a bloody and murdering practice than a fellowly sport'. Despite attempts by Henry VIII and Elizabeth I to suppress the game it still flourished into the eighteenth century when the sport attracted gentry and country folk. The betting stakes on these matches were often high between gentlemen but the prizes for the players of the winning teams were often a few shillings, gloves or a fine new hat for each player.

Campen died out in Suffolk in the late eighteenth century after two men were killed in their struggle during a match at Easton, near Framlingham. A modified game of campen continued with a smaller ball that could be thrown but still had to be carried through the narrow goal of the opposing team, and it was here that there were still fights and jostling. During the nineteenth century, campen was replaced by more gentlemanly, less violent games with clear sets of rules, such as Association Football and Rugby. But local lads having a kick about on the village green would still be known to cry 'camp rules' and their match would be turned into a free-for-all just like the good old days! Camping lands are still remembered in Suffolk but in field names such as Camping Close or in areas of town and villages which retain a name that reflect their past use, such as The Campen at Needham Market.

ALL SORTS OF SPORTS

The Pugilist Championship of All England was fought between Tom Paddock and Harry Broome on 19 May 1856 near Bentley. The match was attended by the great and the good from far and wide, including local luminaries such as Richard Garrett, the Leiston iron founder, and an Indian prince with his entire entourage. In 1856 the gloves were literally off – it was all bare-knuckle fighting, so the achievement is all the more considerable when the match was decided in Paddock's favour after fifty-one rounds.

James Moore (1849–1935), winner of the first Paris-Rouen road race in 1869, who became one of the first international stars of bicycle racing, was born at Long Brackland, near Bury St Edmunds. Moore became an early world champion cyclist when he won the MacGregor Cup in 1872, 1873, 1874, 1875 and 1877 – he retired from racing the same year.

The first match played by Ipswich Town Rugby Football Club by the aid of electric lights was played on the evening of 17 December 1878, between Ipswich and United Suffolk. The electric lights were supplied by Mr Paterson of London and were powered by two of Messrs Ransomes, Sims and Head's patent portable engines that were loaned for the occasion. United Suffolk won the match 5–3.

In 1787, James Potter, the keeper of the Queen's Head, donated a handsome silver cup to be played for between eleven Nayland gentlemen and any team of gentlemen who cared to meet them, on payment of 1s per player.

On 3 May 1758, a wager was laid at Newmarket by a young lady that she would ride 1,000 miles in 1,000 hours. She accomplished her feat in little more than a third of the time.

When Sir Connop Guthrie won the 1936 King's Cup Air Race in his Percival Vego Gull monoplane, he lived at Brent Eleigh Hall.

The earliest recorded mention of a horse racing meet at Ipswich was in 1710 when a Town Purse was run for by 'high mettled racers'.

The Ipswich Races held their last Royal Plate meet in 1883.

The annual Suffolk Walking Festival includes The Discover Suffolk Challenge Walk, a series of five walks which follow the entire length of the Suffolk Coast and Heaths AONB's Suffolk Coast Path and cover almost 70 miles in five days.

Darts World Champion Keith Deller was born in Ipswich in 1959.

The last bull baiting to be held in Ipswich was at Fleece Yard in 1805.

A record-breaking rod-and-line-caught turbot, weighing 28lb 8oz, was caught by Mr J.D. Dorling on Dunwich Beach in 1973.

A halibut weighing 33lb, believed to be the largest caught on a line off the Suffolk coast, was landed by Lowestoft skipper Steve Wightman on his boat *Maximus* in February 2008.

Bungay Marathon was run for their first time on Easter Sunday, 11 April 1982.

SOME BITS ABOUT
IPSWICH TOWN FOOTBALL CLUB

Ipswich Town Football Club was formed as an amateur club after a meeting was held with this purpose in mind at Ipswich Town Hall on Wednesday, 16 October 1878. Thomas Clement Cobbold, MP for Ipswich and member of the famous local brewing family, was unanimously voted president – a post he was delighted to accept and held until his death in 1883.

The original name of the team was Ipswich Association Football Club.

Their first home ground was Broom Hill, Norwich Road, where they played between the years 1878 and 1883. A ground opposite Broom Hill known as Brook's Hall became their next home, where they played until the 1887/8 season. The ground at Portman Road has been their home ever since.

Ipswich played their first match at Broom Hill on Saturday, 26 October 1878 between the Secretary's Team and the Club. Club President Cobbold presented the club a new ball for the match and kicked off at about 3.15 p.m. The teams were well matched, Mr F.G. Bond scored the first goal against the club, but, undaunted, the Club made a number of determined attacks on the Secretary's Team goal and finally Mr A. Edwards scored the first goal for the Club. Two more goals were scored and the match ended as a 2–2 draw.

Ipswich entered for the FA Cup for the first time in 1890.

Ipswich was one of the first football clubs to adopt nets for their goals.

The original pitch the team played on at Portman Road is still in use as their current training area.

Ipswich wore a football shirt with vertical blue and white stripes between 1888 and 1935.

Ipswich Town became a professional team in 1936 after winning the Southern League at their first attempt and were elected to the Football League on 30 May 1938.

The first insignia for Ipswich Town FC was the Ipswich Town coat of arms.

A new club badge based around a heraldic design, including the castellations inspired by the Wolsey Gate and shield reminiscent of the knights of old with the Suffolk Punch horse as its prominent symbol, was designed in 1972 by Mr John Gammage as one of hundreds of competition entries to create a new club badge. The badge was redesigned for the 1995/6 season but still retains all of its traditional themes.

The first permanent floodlights were installed at Portman Road on 16 February 1960.

Sir Alf Ramsey (manager 1955–1963) and Sir Bobby Robson (manager 1969–1982) were both successful managers of Ipswich Town, and statues of both of them have been erected at Portman Road.

Mick Mills holds the record for the most appearances for Ipswich in competitive games (including appearances as substitute), playing in a total of 741 matches between 1966 and 1982. Mick was capped 42 times for England while he was an Ipswich player.

The player to score the most goals in a single season is Leiston-born Ted Phillips who scored 46, including 41 League goals, in the 1956/7 season.

The all-time top Ipswich Town goal scorer is Ray Crawford who played for Ipswich from 1958 to '63 and again in 1965 to '68, scoring a total of 218 goals in competitive professional matches. Ray was also the first Ipswich Town player to be capped for England, in a match against Northern Ireland on 22 November 1961.

The longest-serving manager of Ipswich Town was Scott Duncan who served the club between 1937 and 1955, leading them to victory as Division Three (South) champions 1953/4. The man who was Ipswich Town's manager through the greatest number of games however, was Bobby Robson who managed the club for 709 games between 1969 and 1982.

The youngest ever first-team player was Connor Wickham, who played in a match against Doncaster Rovers on 11 April 2009, just eleven days after his 16th birthday. When he was eventually sold to Sunderland in June 2011, Connor attracted the highest transfer fee for any Ipswich player to that date - £8.10 million.

Sergei Baltacha became the first professional Soviet footballer to play for a British team when he joined Ipswich Town from Dynamo Kiev in 1988.

Ipswich Town had their biggest League victory when they won 7–0 against Portsmouth in a Second Division match on 7 November 1964.

Ipswich suffered their biggest League defeat when they lost 10–1 against Fulham in a First Division match on 26 December 1963.

Today, Ipswich Town's home ground, Portman Road, has a maximum capacity of capacity of 30,311 – the largest capacity of any football stadium in East Anglia.

Ipswich won the FA Cup in 1978 (beating Arsenal 1–0), exactly 100 years after they had been formed as an amateur club.

Ipswich Town's winning FA Cup team of 1978 (eleven starters and one sub) were:

Mick Mills (Captain)
Roger Osborne – the local boy who scored the only and the winning goal.
Paul Cooper
Brian Talbot
Allan Hunter
Kevin Beattie
John Wark
Paul Mariner
David Geddes
Clive Woods
George Burley
Mick Lambert (Substitute)

Ipswich Town has enjoyed the nicknames of the 'Town', the 'Blues' and more recently, the 'Tractor Boys'.

SUFFOLK FOOTBALL LEAGUES IN 1905

Suffolk County Football Association
North Suffolk League
Ipswich and District League
Norfolk and Suffolk League
Ipswich Football Charity Cup

Haverhill and District League
South-East Anglian League
Lowestoft and District League
Lowestoft Borough League

SUFFOLK AMATEUR FOOTBALL CLUBS EXTANT IN 1905

Beccles Caxton Reserves
Barnham
Blundeston
Bramford and District
Brandon
Brantham Crown
Bredfield
Bungay
Bury St Edmunds
Bury St Edmunds Rovers
Campsea Ashe Park
Clare
Clopton & District
Combs Rangers
Corton
Euston Park Rangers
Felixstowe
Framlingham Town
Glemsford
Great Thurlow United
Halesworth
HMS Fisgard
Hadleigh
Haverhill Rovers

Hollesley United
Ipswich Town
Kirkley Albions
Knodishall
Landguard Fort
Lavenham
Leiston
Leiston Rangers
Long Melford
Lowestoft Town
Mildenhall
Melton Asylum
Nayland
Needham Market
Newmarket
Oulton United
Saxmundham
Somerleyton
Southwold Town
Stowmarket
Sudbury United
Woodbridge School
Wrentham
Yoxford

IPSWICH WITCHES

Foxhall stadium was constructed as a purpose-built speedway track in 1950 and the first meeting of the Ipswich Witches Speedway Club was held there in 1951.

In the heyday of the Ipswich Witches, attendances approaching 20,000 were not unknown at Foxhall.

In 1965, the track was resurfaced for stock car racing. An undaunted Mr John Berry built a smaller track inside the stock car circuit and reopened the club in 1969.

The Witches won the Division I Championship in 1975, 1976 and 1984, as well as numerous Knock-Out Cup wins (doing 'The double' in 1976 and 1984).

The Witches won the Elite League Championship, the Knock-Out Cup and the end of season Craven Shield tournament in 1998 and became Premier League Four-Team Champions in 2011.

The current track has a length of 285m.

The track record is 55.4 seconds, achieved by Niels-Kristian Iversen on 5 September 2019.

Stars of Ipswich Witches Speedway Club include:

Syd Clarke
Junior Bainbridge
Tich Read
Peter Moore
John Louis (now the Ipswich Promoter)
Chris Lewis (now Director of Speedway at Ipswich and Mildenhall)
Jeremy Doncaster
Scott Nicholls
Billy Sanders
Birger Forsberg
Dennis Sigalos
John Cook
Olle Nygren
Bert Edwards
Bob Sharp

IPSWICH CYCLISTS

In 1905 there were seven different cycling clubs in Ipswich, namely the
Ipswich Cycle Club, Cruisers, Ramblers, Conservative, Rovers, Early
Closing, Cycling and Recreation Association and St Helens.

SPORT OF KINGS – NEWMARKET FACTS

The potential of Newmarket for equine pursuits was recognised by King James I while he was hunting there in 1605. Indeed, James liked the place so much that he had a palace built there.

The first recorded race to be held at Newmarket took place on 18 March 1622. It was contested between a horse belonging to Lord Salisbury and another belonging to the Marquis of Buckingham. Buckingham's horse won and the Marquis received a prize worth £100 – a considerable sum back in those days.

Charles II built Palace House at Newmarket for his twice yearly visits, when he would bring the entire royal court with him.

The racecourse hosts two of Britain's five horse racing Classics – the 1,000 Guineas and the 2,000 Guineas.

Technically, Newmarket Racecourse has three courses: the Rowley Mile (actually 1 mile and 2 furlongs), the July or Summer Course of 1 mile, and the Round Course. The latter is used once a year for one of the old contests still run there, the Newmarket Town Plate, which was instigated by Newmarket regular King Charles II in 1664 or 1665 (accounts vary).

The Rowley Mile is named after Charles II – it came from the name of the King's favourite hack at Newmarket called Old Rowley, and the name stuck to both horse and king.

In 1666, the Newmarket Town Plate became the first race to be run with a specific set of written rules, which included:

Every rider that layeth hold on, or striketh any of the riders, shall win no plate or prize.

Whosoever winneth the plate or prize shall give to the Clerk of the Course twenty shillings, to be distributed to the poor both sides of Newmarket, and twenty shillings to the Clerk of the Race for which he is to keep the course plain and free from cart roots.

No man is admitted to ride for this prize that is either a serving man or groom.

The Newmarket Plate is the oldest surviving horse race in the world.

The Jockey Club was formed at Pall Mall in London in 1750 and moved soon after to Newmarket, where it leased a plot of land and built a coffee house on the high street. Purchasing the freehold, they then built the magnificent Jockey Club Rooms, where they remained until the 1960s.

The very first 2,000 Guineas race at Newmarket was held on 18 April 1809. The winner was a chestnut horse named Wizard that roamed home to beat seven rivals.

Newmarket was the only racecourse to remain open throughout both world wars and all five Classics were run at the course during those years.

In 1929, Newmarket's July Course was the first to introduce the Tote.

In 1949, the Newmarket 2,000 Guineas was the first ever horse race to use a photo finish camera to help determine the winner.

In 1965, Newmarket's July Course became the first British course to use starting stalls.

THE LEGENDARY FRED ARCHER

Fred Archer was, and remains, a racing legend. Amongst his Classics wins are 6 St Legers, 5 Derbys and 4 Oaks, and out of the total 8,004 races he participated in, he won 2,748. A champion jockey every year from 1874 until his untimely death in 1886 he was truly at the top of his craft. But, tragically, all was not well with Fred Archer. In 1884 his infant son died, and in the same year his wife died following complications during the birth of their daughter. Not only beset with family tragedy, Archer, who was 5ft 10in, fought progressively harder to maintain his weight, and increasingly relied on a strong purgative known as Archer's Mixture. This all proved too much for Fred and in November 1886 he took his life at his home in Newmarket with a pistol.

SUFFOLK CRICKET CLUBS EXTANT IN 1905

Aldeburgh
Beccles Caxton
Beccles College
Bury and West Suffolk
Bury United
Bury St John's
Frasers'
Grundisburgh and Burgh
Hadleigh
Horkesley Park
Ipswich YMCA
Ipswich and East Suffolk
Ipswich Orwell Works
W. & A.J. Turner's (Ipswich)

Ipswich School
Ipswich Northgate School
Ixworth
Lowestoft Town
Nacton
Newmarket All Saints'
Newmarket Cricket Club
Somerleyton
Sudbury
Tattingstone and District
Theobald's Grammar School
Woodbridge School
Woolverstone Park

SUFFOLK STEEL QUOITS

Although there are similar games to be found in other parts of Britain and Europe, the rules and method of play for Suffolk Steel Quoits are unique to the county.

Up to the mid-twentieth century most Suffolk villages and every town had at least one quoits team and many pubs had their own quoits pitch.

The Suffolk Challenge Cup for quoits was first contested in 1888 and the first winners were the Waterside Works of Ipswich.

The most famous of all the Suffolk prizes for quoits is the Silver Cup, first presented by Lord Rendlesham in 1914. It is still competed for today.

Suffolk Steel Quoits flourished until the 1970s then went into decline and most of the old leagues had to fold. Today there are just two leagues – the Hadleigh League and the Stoke by Nayland League – with five teams in each.

Originally the game was played on grass, often on the village green, with the target pins visible above ground. If the villagers did not have the round quoits, they played the game with old horse shoes. The game evolved so that the pitch became one of clay and during the game's height, there would even be 'cleaners' who would clean the quoits with sand or sawdust between each end. A useful helper to players is the 'lighter', who places a small strip of whitepaper within the bed before each throw for the player to aim at.

The basic rules specific to Suffolk Steel Quoits are as follows:

The pitch should be 18 yards long with a clay quoit bed, 2 feet square, enclosed in a wooden frame.

In the lay of this bed a circle of 18 inches is marked around a 5/8 inch diameter hob so it is fully embedded in the clay, its top end flush with the smooth clay surface.

The clay must be of such consistency a well thrown quoit should embed itself at an angle.

Quoits shall not exceed 7¼lb per pair and 7¼ inches in diameter

A single game is played by a minimum of two people. Each player throws two quoits alternately each turn. The players then walk to the other hob, score the end and then standing alongside it, throw the quoits back to the opposite hob.

The player with the quoit nearest to the hob at the end scores one point. The same player will score another point if his second quoit is closer to the hob than any of his opponents points.

A 'ringer' – a quoit that surrounds but does not cover the hob – scores 2 points and is removed from the bed before the next throw. The maximum points possible for any player to score from one end is 4.

A quoit that covers the pin in known as a 'cover' and counts before a 'side-toucher'.

Any quoit on top of a 'cover' cannot count as a 'ringer.'

A quoit that lands on its back is known as a 'woman' or one that lands inclining backwards does not count and is removed.

A quoit that alights 18 inches or more from the hob is deemed a 'no quoit' and withdrawn.

The winner is the first player to achieve 21 points (in League matches this rises to 31 points).

BIG SHOTS

Benacre Hall was regarded as one of the best estates in East Anglia for all-round shooting for most of the nineteenth century. The game books recorded such bags as 704 partridges shot over five days around New Year 1859, and 663 hares shot in five days in 1860. In 1868/9, moreover, 3,803 partridges, 149 woodcock and 1,734 hares were shot, and in the season 1895/6 a total of 5,940 pheasants fell to the guns.

During the nineteenth century, when country houses paid bounties to guns and unarmed individuals who were able to catch or trap examples of rare birds, in order to enhance the houses' collection of taxidermied ornithology, there really were more guns than binoculars watching birds in Suffolk. The birds shot or captured in the country during that time include:

A Golden Eagle shot at Woodbridge in December 1876.
A fine male osprey was caught by a labourer in a trap he set in a tree near Bury St Edmunds in May 1863, another was shot at Thorpe on 16 October 1874 and another 'fine specimen' shot at Redgrave in October 1875.

Male Peregrine falcons were shot near
Bury St Edmunds in December 1878 and
another at Ickworth Church in 1860.
Melins were shot at Aldeburgh in
August 1869, 1871 and 1873.
A sparrowhawk in white plumage was
shot at Culford in 1867 and another
at Fornham St Genevieve in 1868.
Two kites were shot at Ickworth in 1840.
A honey Buzzard was shot at
Somerleyton in the spring of 1854.
A male specimen of Burron's Skua
was shot from a bathing machine
at Aldeburgh in 1860.

A Little Auk was knocked down with a whip at Hollesley in 1850. One was taken in an exhausted state in a pig yard at Broadmere near Troston in 1878 by a boy who put his hat over it. Another was picked up swimming down Abbeygate Street, Bury St Edmunds, during a great storm of rain in 1846.

SLIPPERY PIG

A popular activity on high days and holidays in Suffolk was 'Hunt the Pig'. The tail of the animal would have been cut short some time before the day and allowed to heal, then when the time came it would be greased or soaped up then let loose around the village for the populace to run after. The aim of the game was to catch hold of the poor beast by the stump of its tail without touching any other part, and the person who could keep a good grip on it could claim the pig as their prize.

12

ON
THIS DAY

JANUARY

1 January 1879	John Haythorpe, the Sation Master at Bramford, was commended by the Home Secretary for his services at a fire at The Gables, helping to save several children and a blind lady all through ensuring his station buckets were kept free of ice.
2 January 1922	Fire at the historic Rose & Crown Hotel, Sudbury.
3 January 1879	Opening of Messrs Footman & Co.'s Stay Factory at Stowmarket.
5 January 1830	Explosion at Ipswich Gas Works.
7 January 1904	Funeral of ex-Superintendent John Riches, late East Suffolk Constabulary, at Beccles.
8 January 1879	Ringshall Church reopened after restoration.
9 January 1880	The first steamroller was introduced to Ipswich.
10 January 1812	Ipswich Market Cross and shambles were pulled down.

12 January 1813   Opening of the Bethesda Baptist Chapel,
                    Stowmarket.

14 January 1328   Hurricane winds drove the sea against the spit
                    of land known as the King's Holme at Dunwich
                    and pushed it into the harbour area, effectively
                    rendering it impassable. All trade and revenues
                    simply moved to Walberswick and Dunwich was
                    left to rot.

15 January 1327   Great riot at Bury St Edmunds. The town gates
                    were broken down and the abbey was raided.

17 January 1879   Gas explosion at Mrs Spanton's house on
                    Crown Street, Bury.

18 January 1881   A great snowstorm swept across Suffolk.

19 January 1879   Fire at Orwell Lodge, Ipswich.

22 January 1879   Consecration of the churchyard extension of
                    St Margaret's, Lowestoft.

23 January 1893   A cabmen's shelter was opened on Cornhill,
                    Ipswich.

24 January 1879   In a tragic accident, Alice Mary Wright was run
                    over by the luggage train at Ingate Crossing,
                    Beccles.

25 January 1879   Dedication of the bells of the parish church of
                    Stratford St Mary.

27 January 1868   The new Ipswich Town Hall was opened.

29 January 1879   Opening tea of the Crown and Castle Hotel,
                    Orford.

30 January 1880   A landslip at Felixstowe killed two people.

31 January 1879   Bucklesham Church reopened after restoration.

FEBRUARY

3 February 1879   A piece of stone fell from Ipswich Town Hall, killing a Mr Robert Davey on the spot.

5 February   Jim Smith 'The Ipswich Pedestrian' set out to walk from the Fleece Inn in St Matthew's, Ipswich, to the Bull in Aldgate, London. He completed his pedestrian feat in thirty-three hours.

7 February 1879   Entertainment was held at Yoxford in aid of the Street Gas Lighting Fund.

9 February 1934   The first day of the Wortham Tithe War – the only major Blackshirt action outside London.

11 February 1913   Suffragette leader Mrs Emmeline Pankhurst came to Ipswich.

13 February 1922   Legendary First World War Padre 'Woodbine Willie' – real name Revd Geoffrey Studdart Kennedy MC – visited Ipswich.

20 February 1819   First official day of the Bungay Watch (a localised forerunner of the police force).

21 February 1879   Inquest held at Laxfield into the death of 60-year-old Samuel Monser, who was found dead in a ditch with his overturned cart resting on his body.

22 February 1922   A fog of impenetrable density hung over Ipswich until midday.

25 February 1815   Riots at Gosbeck.

26 February 1901   A celebration lunch was held in honour of the Ipswich Volunteers on their departure to the South African War.

27 February 1879   Telegraph communication at Yoxford and Peasenhall was completed.

28 February 1904   Death of Mr Walter Finch, clerk of Wickham Market parish church for many years.

MARCH

1 March 1688   The Great Fire of Bungay. With the exception of one small street and a few detached houses, the town was reduced to ashes within six hours.

3 March 1904   A drinking trough for cattle at Haverhill was formally handed over on behalf of the donor, Lady Malcom of Poltalloch.

6 March 1909   First march out of the Suffolk Regiment Territorials in Ipswich.

8 March 1879   Funeral of Revd Canon Molyneaux at Sudbury.

14 March 1845   A violent frost occurred in Ipswich.

18 March 1904   The family of James Cutting was accidentally poisoned at Woodbridge.

20 March 1922   Fire at Prentice's Chemical Works, Stowmarket.

21 March 1879   Mr Charles Sankey was elected headmaster of the King Edward VI Grammar School in Bury.

23 March 1812   John and Elizabeth Smith of Cookley were hanged at Ipswich Gaol for the mistreatment and punishment of their children, which eventually killed one of them.

25 March 1889   A fire occured at Packard's Manure Works on Ipswich Quay.

26 March 1800   Suffolk heroine Margaret Catchpole made good her infamous escape from Ipswich Gaol.

28 March 1891   Lyceum Theatre opened on Carr Street, Ipswich.

30 March 1904   The scholars of the Henham and Wangford School celebrated the Viscount Dunwich's first birthday, and the presentation of a school flag by the Earl of Stradbroke.

APRIL

1 April 1916   Zeppelin raid on Suffolk. Seven were killed or fatally wounded at Bury St Edmunds, and five lost their lives in Sudbury.

2 April 1868   The streets of Wickham Market are lit for the first time.

3 April 1879   Coffee and Reading Rooms opened at Long Melford.

4 April 1925   Landguard lighthouse was destroyed by fire and explosion.

7 April 1876   Fire at Bramford Tar Works.

8 April 1763   Richard Ringe and Margery Beddingfield executed as murderer and accomplice on Rushmere Heath near Ipswich. Ringe was hanged but because Mrs Beddingfield was complicit in the murder of her husband, she was executed under the law of petty treason and was burnt at the stake.

9 April 1869   The Ipswich Scientific Society was founded.

10 April 1904   Congregational Sunday Schools opened at Leiston.

11 April 1608   Fire broke out in Bury St Edmunds. Strong winds fanned the flames and the fire consumed 160 dwelling houses plus stores and divers of other buildings resulting in damages to the value of £60,000.

12 April 1818	Stoke Bridge in Ipswich iwas destroyed by flood waters.
13 April 1904	The first Daffodil Show was held under the auspices of the Ipswich and East of England Horticultural Society.
14 April 1879	Foundation stone of a new Congregational Sunday School house at Beccles laid by Mr J.J. Colman MP.
15 April 1915	Zeppelin raid on Henham and Lowestoft. Great damage was caused but fortunately no lives were lost.
16 April 1879	Concert at Barham on behalf of a warming apparatus for the parish church.
18 April 1866	Foundation stone laid for the new Ipswich Town Hall.
19 April 1922	A fire at Trimley Corn Mills resulted in £2,000 of damage.
20 April 1870	George Page, 'The Suffolk Giant' who stood over 7ft tall, died aged 26. He was born and buried at Newbourne.
22 April 1851	George Cant, aged 23, was the last man to be executed at Bury St Edmunds. He had been found guilty of the murder of Elizabeth Payne at Lawshall.
23 April 1800	Servant girl Sarah Lloyd was hanged at Bury St Edmunds for petty treason after she opened the door of her mistress's house to her lover, a thief, who robbed the house.
26 April 1892	Fire at Chequers Inn, Blakenham.
28 April 1914	Suffragettes Evaline Hilda Birkitt and Florence Olivia Tunks burned down the Bath Hotel in Felixstowe.

MAY

1 May 1848	Ipswich Paper Mills Fire, Waterworks Street.
3 May 1758	A wager was laid by a young lady at Newmarket that she would ride 1,000 miles in 1,000 hours. She accomplished her feat in little more than a third of the time.
4 May 1855	The last fair was held on Cornhill in Ipswich.
5 May 1910	Christabel 'Queen of the Mob' Pankhurst spoke on the Suffragette cause for the first time in Suffolk at the Ipswich Corn Exchange.
7 May 1879	Sudden death of Mr W.C. Mason, Head Constable of the Ipswich Borough Police for forty years.
11 May 1904	First concert of the Felixstowe Orchestral Society.
13 May 1911	Lord Haldane opened the new Ipswich Drill Hall for the 1st East Anglian Field Ambulance and the Essex and Suffolk Cyclist Battalion on Woodbridge Road.
14 May 1879	Trial of Sullivan's Patent Wagon Brake at Ipswich.
15 May 1915	An anti-German disturbance occurred on Carr Street, Ipswich.
17 May 1904	First ordinary business meeting of the Eastern Counties Farmers' Co-operative Association at Ipswich.
18 May 1876	A small riot took place at Ipswich between soldiers and civilians. Part of the Borough Police Force, which had been on duty at the racecourse, happened to be riding by; police staves were drawn, the rioters were engaged and, after a brief fracas, were quietened.

19 May 1911	Suffragette demonstration at Woodbridge.
20 May 1909	Newspapers across Britain run the story of the sighting of a mysterious luminous airship off Lowestoft.
21 May 1556	Three martyrs, Thomas Spicer of Winston, John Deny and Edmund Poole, both of Mendlesham, were burnt at the stake at Beccles.
22 May 1893	The *Hearts of Oak* lifeboat was launched at Lowestoft.
24 May 1910	Halley's Comet was seen in the sky above Eye.
25 May 1922	A violent thunderstorm showers Suffolk with giant hailstones.
28 May 1672	The Battle of Solebay off Southwold.
29 May 1898	Twelve motor cars visited Ipswich.
30 May 1923	A fire at Orwell Park Mansion in Ipswich caused £20,000 of damage.
31 May 1911	National hero Lord Kitchener inspects a rally of 600 Boy Scouts on Portman Road.

JUNE

1 June 1902	The Peasenhall Murder. The body of Rose Harsent was discovered, her throat cut and laying in a pool of blood at Providence House in Peasenhall. William Gardener, a man believed to have been her lover, was tried twice for the murder but the juries could not agree and the case against him was declared *nolle prosequi*.

3 June 1665	Naval battle fought off Lowestoft between Charles II's English Fleet and the Dutch, between three in the morning and seven in the evening. The Dutch were completely routed, with the loss of eighteen ships captured and fourteen sunk or burnt to the loss of just one English ship.
4 June 1879	Inquest at East Bergholt into the death of James Mansfield, a mail cart driver who died after accidentally falling out of his cart.
6 June 1903	Horse trams ceased running in Ipswich.
8 June 1904	The croquet lawn at the Lower Arboretum at Ipswich was opened for its first season.
10 June 1879	The first of a series of promenade concerts was held at Stowmarket.
11 June 1845	The first train ran between Ipswich and Colchester.
12 June 1381	The Peasant's Revolt in Suffolk broke out in Liston, led by John Wrawe.
13 June 1908	'The Masked Man', real name Harry Bensley of Thetford, visited Ipswich. He was involved in a wager, whereby if he successfully wore a mediaeval knights' helmet while pushing a perambulator around the world he would collect the veritable winnings of £21,000.
14 June 1883	Death of Edward Fitzgerald (1809–1883). Known to the world for his version of the *Rubaiyat of Omar Khayyam*, he spent nearly all his life at Boulge and Woodbridge.
15 June 1881	The new Ipswich sewerage system was opened and a luncheon was held in the covered reservoir.
17 June 1917	Zeppelin L.48 came down onto land belonging to Holly Tree Farm, Theberton.

18 June 1904   Alexandra Park in Ipswich was opened by the
                      Mayor, Mr Fred Bennett.

20 June 1898   Penny omnibuses began services in Ipswich.

22 June 1778   Smugglers Robert Debney and William Cooper
                      died from asphyxiation in their underground
                      hideaway after succumbing to the vapours of
                      the horse manure that covered and disguised it.
                      They are buried side by side in Tunstall
                      churchyard.

24 June 1533   Death of Mary Rose Tudor, the youngest sister of
                      Henry VIII to live past childhood and the princess
                      who was to become Queen of France following
                      her marriage to Louis XII. Her body was interred
                      in the Abbey of Bury St Edmunds and moved for
                      safekeeping to St Mary's Church after the abbey
                      was dissolved in 1540.

25 June 1879   A fire at Stratford St Andrew causes the partial
                      destruction of four cottages.

29 June 1885   Lowestoft Pier is badly damaged by fire.

30 June 1879   The fifty-fourth anniversary dinner of the Ipswich
                      Shipwrecked Seamen's Society at the White Elm.

JULY

1 July 1898   Felixstowe town railway opened.

3 July 1831   Pioneer photographer Robert Howlett, famous
                      for his iconic photographs of Isambard Kingdom
                      Brunel and Crimean War veterans, was born at
                      Theberton.

4 July 1917   Eighteen German Gotha Bombers attacked
                      Felixstowe and Harwich, killing nine and leaving
                      nineteen wounded at the Royal Naval Air Service
                      base.

7 July 1879	The Yarmouth and Lowestoft fish train accident, near Halesworth Station.
10 July 1848	A Portuguese diver walked underwater from Harwich to Shotley Gate.
11 July 1904	Great Welnetham Church reopened after restoration.
12 July 1868	A fire at Stowmarket destroyed eighteen cottages.
13 July 1903	Railway lines opened between Lowestoft and Great Yarmouth.
16 July 1904	The first athletic sports promoted exclusively for the working boys of Ipswich were held on the Portman Road ground.
18 July 1904	The Great Eastern Railway service of motor buses commenced running between Southwold and Lowestoft.
19 July 1825	*The Times* published a report on huckster Isaac Stebbings, aged 67, being swum at Wickham Skeith to discover if he was a wizard.
21 July 1897	Streets in Ipswich were rapidly flooded and two boys were killed by a single strike of lightning.
22 July 1921	Fire at Sizewell Hall.
23 July 1904	A Dowie (Pentecostal) baptism was conducted on the beach at Felixstowe.
25 July 1879	The organ at Little Waldringfield Church was unveiled.
29 July 1911	A massive gathering of over 1,000 Juvenile Foresters (Ancient Order of Foresters) at Wherstead.

30 July 1584   'Old ladie Ichingham' was buried in Barsham churchyard, having died after reputedly reaching the age of 110 years.

AUGUST

1 August 1898   The Yoxford wedding tragedy.

4 August 1577   'Demonic' black dogs burst into churches at Bungay and Blythburgh and created havoc during a huge thunderstorm.

5 August 1842   The Ipswich Watch Committee undertook drastic measures and dismissed the entire Ipswich Borough Police.

6 August 1879   The Greyhound Inn at Westhall was destroyed by fire.

8 August 1815   First steam vessel on the River Orwell.

10 August 1854   The Parochial School at Capel St Mary was struck by lightning, which killed three children.

11 August 1828   Execution of William Corder, the 'Red Barn Murderer', in front of Bury St Edmunds prison.

12 August 1915   The Zeppelin L.10, under the command of Oberleutnant Friedrich Wenke, dropped four high-explosive and twenty incendiary bombs on Woodbridge, killing six and injuring twenty-four.

14 August 1909   The first taxi appeared on the Cornhill cab rank, Ipswich.

15 August 1879   Inquest at Drinkstone on Henry James Rose, who died from inflammation of the bowels, accelerated by rough usage.

16 August 1785	Mary Haselton of Bury St Edmunds was repeating her vespers while in prayer when she was instantaneously killed by a flash of lightning.
17 August 1904	The Independent Martyrs Memorial was unveiled at the Congregational Church on Whiting Street, Bury St Edmunds.
18 August 1900	Mr A. Branch was killed in Ipswich by the explosion of a rocket.
22 August 1879	Colours of the 2nd Battalion, 12th Regiment, were deposited in St Mary's Church in Bury.
23 August 1581	John Browne of Halesworth died at the aged of 80 years and 25 weeks. His commemorative brass in the church reads: 'He had by his only wyffe, with whom he lived 54 years and ffive monethes, six sonnes and ten daughters. He hadd also 65 grandchildren, of who 54 were living at the day of his decease.'
27 August 1924	Robert Stanmore, the last of fifty-seven Ipswich Crimean War veterans, died aged 98.
28 August 1904	James Smith, a bricklayer's labourer at Long Melford, died from shock caused by a wasp stinging his tongue.

SEPTEMBER

3 September 1911	The Sunday newspaper boys strike in Ipswich.
4 September 1879	Bildestone Church reopened after restoration.
5 September 1898	Barnum & Bailey's circus paid its first visit to Ipswich.

6 September 1660	Broad Street in Bury St Edmunds was infested by thousands of spiders of a reddish colour.
7 September 1903	Buffalo Bill's Wild West Show visited Ipswich.
8 September 1905	General William Booth, founder of The Salvation Army, visits Ipswich.
9 September 1822	The London-Ipswich mail coach was carrying a clerk from Alexander & Company whose task was to deliver £30,000 worth of the bank's own £10, £5 and £1 notes to its Ipswich office. When the coach arrived at Ipswich the box was found to have been tampered with and when opened proved to have been emptied! The crime remains an unsolved enigma.
10 September 1515	Thomas Wolsey, son of an affluent Ipswich butcher, was created a Cardinal.
12 September 1894	The Darsham Railway Disaster, in which two platelayers were killed.
13 September 1893	For a wager of £15–£20, William Whale of London attempted to run from London to Great Yarmouth via Ipswich. His attempt was to be staged over two days of twelve hours each but sadly he failed by about two hours.
14 September 1904	Celebration of the centenary of St Luke's Lodge of Freemasons at Ipswich.
15 September 1904	Fire at Atterton's engineering works in Haverhill.
19 September 1907	A fire caused £10,000 of damage at the Lowestoft Box Company.
20 September 1929	Aviator Sir Alan Cobham visited Felixstowe.
22 September 1557	Heretic Revd John Noyes was executed by burning at the stake at Laxfield.

24 September 1879   The Southwold railway was opened.

26 September 1866   Ranson, the 'Suffolk Stag', completed his walk from Ipswich to London and back in thirty-five hours and forty-two minutes.

27 September 1904   Inquest at Stowmarket into the death of railway porter Percy W. Clouting who was cut to pieces while attempting to cross the line in front of an express train.

29 September 1908   The Mid-Suffolk Railway, Haughley and Laxfield was opened.

30 September 1914   Recruits for war service from Suffolk exceeded 10,000 in less than eight weeks.

OCTOBER

1 October 1887   Revd William Meymott Farley, Rector of Cretingham, was murdered in his bed by his cut-throat razor-wielding Curate Revd A.E. Gilbert-Cooper. Found 'guilty but of unsound mind', Gilbert-Cooper was sent to Broadmoor Prison Asylum for the rest of his life.

2 October 1879   Fire aboard SS *Ransome* at Ipswich.

3 October 1904   Mrs Dorothy Waddington of Fornham St Martin was killed by an accidental fall from her bicycle.

7 October 1927   Stoke Park Ipswich, given to the town by Alderman W.F. Paul was opened to the public by Prince Henry (later the Duke of Gloucester).

8 October 1880   Horse trams ran for the first time in Ipswich from Cornhill to the railway station.

12 October 1827   Mr Green made an ascent in his balloon from a meadow near Ipswich Gas Works.

13 October 1879	The new gas holder at Woodbridge was completed.
14 October 1904	First autumn horse sale at Ipswich under the auspices of the Suffolk Horse Society.
15 October 1825	Madame Tussaud brought her travelling exhibition of wax figures to Bury Fair.
17 October 1895	Three African chiefs visited Ipswich.
18 October 1859	Posters announced that a man would walk on the River Orwell from Stoke Bridge to the Griffin pub. Thousands assembled to watch the feat only to discover it was all a hoax.
21 October 1914	The first batch of returned wounded servicemen arrived in Ipswich and Broadwater.
25 October 1905	The first dog show of the Suffolk Kennel Association was held at the Ipswich Drill Hall.
26 October 1909	Reydon hit national headlines after a massive gale blew a French couple in a hot air balloon 800 miles from Nancy in Lorraine across the North Sea to eventually land near Reydon Grove.
30 October 1757	Admiral Edward Vernon of Orwell Park, hero of the Battle of Portobello, known to the sailors in the British Navy as 'Old Grog', died. He is buried at Nacton Church.

NOVEMBER

3 November 1904	The great violinist Jan Kubelik performed at Ipswich.
5 November 1911	The grandstand at Portman Road collapsed during a gale.

6 November 1914   Departure of the 4th Battalion, Suffolk Regiment, for service in France.

8 November 1886   Fred Archer, described as 'the best all-round jockey the Turf has ever seen', had become severely depressed and shot himself in the head at his home in Newmarket.

9 November 1908   Elizabeth Garrett Anderson was elected Mayor of Aldeburgh – the first female mayor in England.

10 November 1879   Henry Bedingfeld was sentenced to death for the murder of Eliza Rudd at Ipswich.

11 November 1879   Opening of the the Reading Rooms built by Sir Edward Kerrison at Hoxne.

14 November 1905   The first motor car fatality in Suffolk occurred when Mr A.L. Staines was killed by a motor car on Wherstead Road, Ipswich.

18 November 1879   Destructive fire at Loudham Hall.

20 November 870   Martyrdom of St Edmund at Hoxne.

22 November 1904   First Annual Exhibition of the Ipswich Camera Club.

24 November 1908   Suffragette Sylvia Pankhurst spoke in the Public Hall in Ipswich.

25 November 1925   Powerful tides damage the sea wall around Felixstowe.

28 November 1900   Three were killed in an explosion at the Trimley Powder Works.

30 November 1902   A fire caused £5,000 worth of damage at Tollemache's Brewery on Brook Street, Ipswich.

DECEMBER

1 December 1885 Rioting occured during polling day for an election at Long Melford.

2 December 1878 East Bergholt Village Club opened.

3 December 1910 Extensive flooding in Ipswich after fifty hours of rain.

4 December 1922 The Ipswich Boys' Club was formed by the police.

5 December 1903 Suffolk County Chess association formed at a meeting of the Ipswich Chess Club.

7 December 1899 Aldeburgh lifeboat disaster. Struck by a heavy curling breaker, the lifeboat capsized and six brave local lifeboatmen lost their lives.

9 December 1878 The 105th Anniversary tea at Stoke Green Baptist Chapel in Ipswich.

11 December 1878 First display of electric light in Ipswich.

15 December 1903 The first Aldeburgh Sprat Dinner was held.

16 December 1903 The Martyrs Memorial was unveiled in Christchurch Park in Ipswich, by the Dean of Canterbury.

17 December 1903 Inquest at East Suffolk and Ipswich Hospital on John Catchpole, who died from an injury caused by falling from a pair of stilts.

20 December 1913 Pretty's corset girls go on strike in Ipswich – for three hours.

21 December 1903 The Production of Power from Refuse was discussed at Ipswich Engineering Society.

22 December 1810	The foundation stone was laid for the old Ipswich cattle market.
24 December 1892	The Barnby Train Disaster. The Lowestoft train smashed into the Beccles train at Barnby. The wreckage was horrific; many were injured but only two deaths occurred as a result of the crash.
26 December 1878	Funeral of Band Sergeant Stimpson of the 3rd Suffolk Rifle Volunteer Corps at Woodbridge.

The destination for history
www.thehistorypress.co.uk